HOW TO DEAL WITH TRAUMA FROM PEOPLE AND THRIVE IN WOKE TIMES

HOW TO DEAL WITH TRAUMA FROM PEOPLE AND THRIVE IN WOKE TIMES

An Insightful Guide on Navigating Life in Modern Times

Tariq Ahad

Published by: Tariq Ahad

Published: 2024

Title: How To Deal With Trauma From People And Thrive In Woke Times

Author: Tariq Ahad

ISBN: 978-629-99209-0-8

Cover Design: Tariq Ahad

Printed by: Amazon KDP

For comments or inquiries please contact: howtodealwithtrauma@gmail.com

Instagram:

Synopsis

People today are dealing with new challenges in life which previous generations did not face. Job losses during a pandemic, increased divorce rates and unaffordable housing have contributed to increased stress and depression plaguing modern society. We are told to take pills and mask our symptoms while moral values crumble and crime rates increase. This book provides an insightful guide on navigating life in modern woke times. Overcome your past trauma, become financially independent and improve your relationship with your partner. Learn practical methods of dealing with stressful people and situations around you, while protecting yourself from those who try to drain your mental health and resources. Using innovative and unconventional methods, we can become emotionally empowered individuals and build safe communities.[1]

Dedicated to every innocent soul suffering from injustice and oppression. Wishing you strength and peace so that you may thrive.

Table of Contents

Chapter 1: Trauma, Stress and Depression in Daily Life

Many people experience cycles of emotions through life. There are happy moments such as graduation, joyful occasions such as weddings and memorable events such as birthdays, a first kiss or finishing an exciting project you are really proud of. Sadly, there are also many painful experiences in life. It can be in the form of physical health issues, mental scars from a bad breakup or grief one has never before experienced in their life, such as from the death of a loved one.

This book will focus on the negative emotions, causes and effects, as well as how to avoid stress altogether. It will also provide insight on how to cope with trauma one might face in life. When we take into account all variables, one may conclude that the majority of our stress and sadness in life are caused by dealing with other individuals. We as humans are social beings designed to communicate and interact with others in our species. This is why some of the most hardened criminals are subjected to solitary confinement, to remove social interaction as a form of punishment. We can look to the animal kingdom to find that many mammals and primates behave alike in nature. Travelling in groups and mating among their own kind, we all long for companionship. Interactions with others can stimulate both good hormones as well as bad feelings inside us all. Monkeys groom themselves but can also fight amongst each other. Some birds and fish build intricate displays to attract a mate, only to be rejected. Likewise, we as humans do things to attract affection from others and often times it will either go unnoticed or be unappreciated.

We make the effort to look good, dress good and smell good to earn interest and admiration. We yearn for others to appreciate and like us, not only through our looks, but also in our speech, degrees, interests, achievements, possessions, status and character. However, from time to time, we may be trying our best in life to do good and trying to be honest and kind to others, only to find that some jerk will try to steal our recompense by copying our schoolwork assignment, taking credit for that work presentation or stealing your girlfriend while you were working late hours to save for a house down payment. It may start in school when the bully steals our lunch money. Or it may even begin before that, with parents who are selfish and abusive. Whatever the cause, old or young, it can affect our health.

Experiencing trauma from a young age such as six-years-old, can greatly affect a person's mental health even into their adulthood. This is especially true if the suffering persists for a prolonged number of years consistently, without any intervention or alleviation. For the example of child abuse, often times the child is left alone and helpless, not knowing where to turn. The abusive parents themselves may threaten the child to stop feeding them, or present horror stories to scare the child from going to outsiders or reporting the matter to the authorities. The child may fear living on the streets or being put in a more abusive home if they were to tell a relative or an authoritative figure. This abuse can often make the abuser feel entitled to continue, as they are not brought to justice and feel powerful over the child. It is similar to how many people with guns were able to take advantage and make slaves of others, while taking their land so many years ago, and still today in some regions of the world. This infringement on basic human rights not only leaves life-long scars on the victim, but it also empowers the abuser to continue their abusive behaviour without any remorse. This can be related to many cases in society.

There are documentations of soldiers invading lands and raping women, mentioning of how the soldiers appreciated the docile nature of women from certain countries. It can be similar to being in an abusive marriage, where one feels overpowered and overwhelmed, to the point where they feel forced to just shut up and take the abuse. Regardless if it is a child, a woman or a man, this is of course not something that should be considered acceptable, but it happens every single day to millions around the world. I often say that I think the gun was the worse invention ever created. The reason is that it gives one person instant and undeniable power and control over another person or group of people, regardless of whether that person is good or bad. It allows people to rape women, rob people of their possessions and conquer lands. It takes a lot more effort and skill to aim a bow and arrow rather than pull a trigger.

Regardless if someone is using a gun to intimidate and overpower you, or if they simply are in a higher authoritative position or more muscular than you are, bullying and imposing on the rights of others is wrong. Yet it happens. So, what does this cause to their victims? Well, aside from suffering instant pain such as a young girl's hymen breaking while being raped, or an old man suffering a concussion and broken ribs from being mugged by a group of teenagers; these incidents engrave a very negative experience in the person's memory which cannot simply be erased. We must come to realize that in life, not everyone will reflect the same attributes that we put forth. Often times people try to live by sayings such as "You get what you give"[2] and "Forgive and forget." But unfortunately, these phrases may not often hold true entirely. Yes, in general, if you are a positive, honest, caring individual, you may attract friends and acquaintances that appreciate and reflect similar characteristics. As well, forgiveness can lead to a more peaceful and fruitful life. However, we must be aware and acknowledge, that there are also people who will feed off of another person's innocent and kind nature, to benefit themselves. These are the ones who will lie, cheat and steal to trick others into getting what they desire by using people. Unfortunately, some of us do not have a strong social or family support backing to help protect us from such people. Therefore, we must learn to cope and protect ourselves.

When someone does not have love in their life at all, such as from parents, a romantic partner, or children, then that person may be classified by society as "psycho" later in life based on their behaviour. They may be lonely without any daily social interactions. They might have lost their spouse, or never been married and have no children. They may feel as though they have nothing to lose, so they can become violent and dangerous when someone steals from them, physically harms them, or otherwise takes advantage of them. They place high value on their material possessions because they have no family to love. So, they take it very personally when someone steals from them or damages their property, similar to if someone were to harm your family.

When a person experiences daily stress while living in a fast-paced society, the stress can build up each day until they reach their breaking point. Sometimes one major negative event can push them over the edge, where that person might explode in front of their co-workers and yell in frustration at their boss. People will think that the person is crazy and gossip about how they seemed so quiet then suddenly snapped. He or she may then be required to attend therapy for a time period suggested by the Human Resources department at their workplace.

Many of us are born very alike, as healthy babies, with empty minds, waiting to be filled with knowledge and disposition in this big new world. However, depending on parental upbringing and the environmental challenges one faces in life, some may grow to be happy, successful and healthy individuals. While others may become distraught, angry and pessimistic. Society will then unfairly treat people differently, based on their inherent personality and attributes, which they attained from their upbringing.

One couple may have a teenaged son, and use him for financial gain, by demanding his salary from his part-time job, and forcing him to do chores instead of allowing him to study mechanical engineering. His life and status in society, will be different than a child who was allowed to accomplish things that he worked for in his life. One son may become a successful automotive engineer, and the other may end up working in a call center, and be labelled as psycho by his co-workers when he yells at his boss. The child who was not given a fair chance in life, will feel as though his potential is not being fulfilled by working in a call center. He will feel frustrated and potentially blame his parents, but his co-workers will not know his story, and they will simply label him as psycho.

Extensive abuse and loneliness can impact a person psychologically, to the point where it affects the prefrontal cortex of their brain, and they no longer consider the legal consequences of retaliating. Stress from other people can literally make a person go crazy. A person may lack physical human comfort such as hugs,[3] which can have healing capabilities if they were to experience it. This can be observed in human behaviour, as well as with animals where they comfort each other. People who lack a physical bond or connection with others, may be more sensitive and obsessive over a matter when another person wrongs them. People are social beings and need love in order to get over things quicker. Without love, some may never get over a traumatic event from their past, which may drain their mental energy thinking about it every single day for the rest of their lives.

A growing concern in modern society among adult men is the lack of physical touch and love from others.[4] Many men lead lonely, isolated lives, and this problem is growing as the term "incel" becomes more mainstream. Unfortunately, such men are often not very attractive to women, live alone, and thus are touch deprived. Women whom would once seek an average man working an average salary, are now becoming more independent with the modern feminist movement. Many of these women believe in not needing a man in their lives, aside from using his sperm should they wish to conceive a child.

For the millions of men who end up in their thirties, forties or later, without being in a romantic relationship and having no close companion in their life, an animal companion may be helpful in such cases. Many men can go months without a hug from anyone, while lacking chemical brain stimulation of endorphins and oxytocin to help them overcome the daily stresses they face dealing with others. This can cause them to develop health issues over time, and can lead to being awkward in society when interacting with people in a social environment, especially after a prolonged time of not doing so.

Numerous men have been hurt by slander, violence against them and insults which they must deal with alone. Some men reach the point where they do not want to be bothered anymore, and prefer to live in isolation to maintain their peace and sanity. Not having the comfort of another human to console you, can cause you to have built up rage and become violent towards others who may hurt you in future. Yet, some will view these individuals as weak and an easy target, so people will try to take advantage of them and hurt them. When people in society take advantage of others who were harmed unjustly previously without recompense; the person being taken advantage of may take the abusive behaviour, then have it build up inside of them until they retaliate. When they do retaliate, many who have not been through the same trauma, may say that they went too far in terms of the punishment they imposed on to the person who abused, robbed, slandered or otherwise wronged them. This is why, as a society we need to understand and acknowledge the growing struggles that some people, primarily men, face, which has not yet been recognized.

Many laws prevent men from being able to protect themselves against things such as slander from women. It is easier for people to take the side of a lying woman and ruin an innocent man's life, rather than stand up against the woman and question her outlandish accusations. Society rarely will defend the innocent man. This is due in part because many men have taken advantage of women throughout history. Women should always be cautious of believing their girlfriends who may be lying with mischievous intent. She may speak ill about a certain guy to keep you away from him, then she will sleep with that same guy behind your back. Your female friend may be jealous of a great guy, such as if you like him or if he likes you. Then she may slander his name to ruin his reputation out of jealousy. If she cannot be happy then why should you, right? Some women will even encourage you to divorce your husband so that she can have him for herself. Always give a person a chance in life to get to know them, even after you may hear something really bad about them which you have not witnessed for yourself. Just because everyone says something is true, does not mean it really happened, and you will not know that person unless you take the time to give them a chance and know them. They may turn out to be a really kind and soft-hearted person you end up marrying or becoming best friends with in life. People will always try to bring a person down when they reach the top, primarily out of jealousy.

Unfortunately, in today's society when a woman says unconfirmed allegations of a man, women will naturally be united and stick together. Meanwhile, simp guys will often take the girl's side, especially if she is attractive. This is because guys are often sexually aroused, and will lie if it means they get a chance to sleep with a girl. This "hate all men and believe all women" behaviour, creates further societal division between men and women. It deteriorates the family structure of a society, which can be seen through the increased divorce rates happening today.

This biasness it is now used strategically in Western society by some deceiving women to their advantage, where they know that the justice system will likely take their side and believe them, without any actual solid evidence. It has shifted from where women were once scared to come forward for actual occurrences of sexual assault and harassment. To now many lying women coming forward with totally false allegations for fame or fortune after a guy has become rich or famous. Even the Prime Minister of a certain Western country has encouraged this behaviour, by stating that we must believe and support these women when they come forward, leaving no chance for an innocent man to defend himself.[5] The woman often has much to gain, and nothing to lose from making false allegations. Typically, if a man is later proven innocent, there is no repercussions or accountability for the woman for her behaviour and lying.

If you are faced with this type of traumatic experience of being wrongfully accused as a man, it may be difficult to defend yourself, so you may need to look into options for your future. This may include a change of lifestyle, within an environment, where the culture aligns with your values. For example, many conservative countries have strict laws against men and women interacting alone together outside of marriage. This practically eliminates the potential for any misconduct. Many people in Western countries may consider this as extremely precautious. However, the cases of rape, sexual assault, theft and other crimes with harsh punishment, are often far lower than compared to many Western countries, where dozens of violent attacks and car jackings happen on a daily basis.[6,7] This is due to poor enforcement of laws and weak penalties, which favour the criminals instead of the victims in some Western countries.[8]

Unfortunately, for decades a very high number of women have faced immoral, disgusting behaviour from men in private and in public around the world. Women are typically of a smaller built stature than men and physically weaker than men. Hence, an average sized man can overpower an average sized woman with ease. Therefore, it is very difficult for a woman to comfortably defend herself from a man who is trying to take advantage of her sexually. This is why, when a woman is cheated on, she may do something such as scratch your car, because that is the only way she can retaliate against you, since you are physically stronger than her. Some strong men may then call the physically weaker woman psycho. Though in reality, he is the one whose behaviour was disgusting. He is the one who cheated or sexually assaulted her, and her actions were her way of defending herself against him.

Typically, most men think about sex multiple times a day, and most men lack the self-control and ethical behavioural teachings to respect women. Many men will try to sleep with a girl they find attractive if they have the opportunity, even if she is married. In countries with an unjust legal system, many men have taken advantage of women, and many unreported sexual assaults have taken place. This behaviour still unfortunately occurs today, affecting women in countries such as India.[9] Men have raped women all around the world throughout history, and this can cause an extremely traumatizing, life-long, lasting effect on a woman. A brief, hormonal, impulsive action to relieve a man's sexual desire, can devastate and ruin a young woman's life, to the point where she could debate suicide to end the trauma. Later in life, the woman may not want her husband to have a beard or wear a certain cologne, because it reminds her of her step-father raping her as a child. Where legally possible, as a woman, you can consider carrying pepper spray or another impactful deterrent to stop a man before he commits the act that can ruin your life.

Rape is one of the most horrific things you can do to a person. Some women have been kidnapped, then held hostage in a basement, while being used as a sex slave for years by their rapist. The men who commit such immoral acts, should of course be punished for their actions. Unfortunately, this life is not perfect, and many instances of rape and other horrific crimes have gone unpunished. However, as we embark on modern times with women voicing their concerns, accusing innocent men of something they did not do is not the answer. Doing so will further divide a society, causing a slower pace towards finding a solution. When a woman falsely accuses a man of something he did not do, it makes it harder to believe real cases of sexual abuse when women come forward in future. It also makes it harder to believe the woman who lied, should she face an actual occurrence of sexual assault in future.

When a society claims to stand up for women's rights, they need to show action in meaningful ways, which prevent rape and other sexual assault occurrences from happening. Forcing biological females to share a washroom with stronger, biological males who identify as females, causes many biological females to feel unsafe and uncomfortable. Washrooms are private settings which are not monitored by security cameras, and this further complicates issues surrounding women's rights. As well, this impacts the LGBTQ community, by giving them a bad reputation for making biological women feel uncomfortable. We need solutions which satisfy and respect all parties involved with such matters, while being understanding of past issues that have occurred, such as women being impacted by serial rapists throughout history.

For certain countries such as Canada, which acknowledge the LGBTQ community, society can respect this group, but also respect women's rights at the same time. A separate, additional washroom could be created to accommodate people who were biologically born males, but went through a transition and now identify themselves as females; while retaining basic male biology such as the inability to go through menstruation, as well as being unable to naturally conceive a child and give birth. This would allow biological males who identify as females, to use the toilet without being forced to use the men's washroom, while allowing biological females to feel safe while they go about their business. For countries where the LGBTQ community is not recognized, the laws and cultural beliefs of these countries must also be respected and abided by. Therefore, forcing one's belief of transgenderism for example, on a conservative society with laws against it, should not be encouraged nor tolerated.

Some people feel stressed and depressed on a daily basis, and live their lives thinking about a traumatic experience that they went through years, if not decades ago. They end up living unfulfilled lives and never accomplish what they want to in life, because their mind is consumed with re-living past trauma, or thinking of things related to it. Some people who experienced traumatic events such as being raped at a young age, or having their life savings taken from them before they were able to enjoy it, feel helpless and trapped. These victims often feel as though they have no one to turn to for help, as their trust in humanity has been severely broken, occasionally numerous times by numerous people including their own family. This feeling causes them to build up walls in their mind to protect themselves from being hurt or taken advantage of again.

This action of building up barriers and not trusting anyone, can also prevent assistance from people who would otherwise be willing and wanting to help them overcome their traumatic experiences. However, the ones who may wish to genuinely help without depending on a salary, are often few. Most humans have many selfish personality traits and could not care to sacrifice a significant amount of their own time and energy to help others. Paid professionals are working in a job which pays their bills, implementing tactics on their patients which they were taught to perform in their secular studies through lectures and textbooks. Many have not lived through the same traumatic scenarios themselves to be able to truly relate to some victims. Professionals are trained to follow protocol, such as recommending prescription medication.[10]

When faced with unique, previously undocumented scenarios, most professionals are inexperienced to manage it properly, and in some cases, may doubt your account as to if what you say actually happened or not. As an example, some have been declared medically dead, only to come back to life minutes later, explaining of things that they saw while being declared medically dead.[11] You know yourself better than most people, and in many instances, you know what you need to make yourself heal and recover better than most people would know. Sometimes, you may need someone to love, or just a hug and a friend to talk to. In other cases, you need your money back that was taken from you, and no amount of counselling will satisfy you to move forward from this until you learn to cope and accept it, or recover your money.

Listen to your body, and use your common sense and own knowledge and reasoning. Even with money, some financial experts may manage your investment portfolio and cause you to lose hundreds of thousands of dollars. Health experts may recommend an ergonomic chair for your scoliosis which causes your back pain to worsen. Yet, you may select a specific chair in a store which you know would help you, and you will immediately feel your back crack into place and feel relief, as your back and neck pain dissipate. Your throbbing headaches related to your spinal issues may also improve with the chair you selected using your own judgement. Experts may argue telling you that the chair you selected is incorrect. However, they are not experiencing what you have experienced for years or decades, and they do not know what you are feeling.

If your health situation worsens based on following expert recommendations, they are seldom held responsible and you will have no recourse, as they are protected by their liability waiver which you were forced to sign before undergoing their treatment plan. If you are not sure what you need however, then the experts may be helpful in guiding you to what may improve your situation. Use caution when the first question asked is whether or not you have health insurance, as health care is a multibillion-dollar industry. Companies will often want to financially benefit from you, even if it means that they must use dishonest business practices. For example, if you know you are taking good care of your teeth, and your dentist recommends several fillings for cavities when you feel no pain. You may want to get a second opinion from another dentist prior to proceeding. It may be that you have no cavities, and your dentist is lying to fraudulently acquire money from you and your insurance company.[12]

When people intentionally harm others, it can leave the victim with feelings of pain, regret, anger, and ongoing mental suffering which can last a lifetime. It can even cause the death of the one who was harmed, through suicide or health related issues. The perpetrator of the immoral act will often move on with their life, not having any care or understanding of the immense impact their negative actions had on their victim.

Sometimes rich people harm poor people in life, such as in a drunk driving related car crash. The wealthy drunk driver may be able to afford to pay their way through the legal system, such as hiring a well-respected and successful lawyer, which the poor victim would not be able to afford. Thus, the victim would not receive proper compensation. The driver who may have injured or killed their victim may not face any significant punishment for their offense, which has cost an innocent person their life.

In some instances such as with rape victims, they can develop post-traumatic stress disorder (PTSD), which can leave them re-living the scenario in their heads, causing ongoing emotional stress, insomnia and physical issues such as heart disease. It is difficult to simply forgive and forget, and just move on, as so many people advise the victims to do. It never happened to them personally, so they cannot comprehend the unimaginable pain and suffering the victim goes through. Many may lose a loved one when they are killed, or miss out on their opportunity to get married when their name is slandered. Or miss out on buying a house or investing in their future when they are robbed of their life savings. The people telling victims to simply live and let live and move on, are often those who have not experienced anything nearly as traumatic as the victims have experienced. For many people, the worst that has happened to them was having a boyfriend/girlfriend cheat on them. These people are mentally weak, and do not provide much valuable advice or insight for the ones who have experienced severe trauma.

There is no peace without justice, and many judicial systems offer little resolution for cases which fall outside of the legal scope or cannot be easily proven. The stress of trying to fight for justice can sometimes be enough to make the victim suffer even more psychological trauma, which can lead to them fainting and giving up in life. Sometimes even just thinking of the stressful trauma can make a person experience vertigo or fall ill, causing them to avoid dealing with remedying the problem in any way. These feelings are amplified for people who have experienced severe trauma, or for some elderly people. Therefore, it may seem healthier and easier for them to just let the person get away with the crime committed upon them. The legal framework's solution in some countries, would be for the victim to attend therapy sessions, instead of targeting the root cause of their mental illness. In order to move forward as a society, we need to look at fair ways to compensate victims when they are affected by trauma caused by others. Many great civilizations will fall when the rights of the innocent are stripped away, and privilege is given to criminals who abuse law abiding citizens. This can cause many good people to turn psycho. Let's try and prevent this shall we?

America for example, is the only developed country in the world that faces high rates of gun violence through mass shootings. Many people argue that this is due to the Second Amendment of the US Constitution, stating that gun violence in American is attributed directly and solely due to high rates of gun ownership in the country among citizens. However, there are several other countries around the world with high gun ownership rates, which do not face anywhere near to the high rates of gun violence experienced in America.[13] In fact, some might argue that those other countries are often very safe, with both minor and major crimes being kept to a minimum.

So why is it that a world leader with one of the highest GDP and most advanced military such as the US, is faced with the challenge of still not being able to control gun violence? Why is it that students are trained with songs and active shooter drills, on what to do if their school is taken over by a lone gunman on a killing spree? Why is it, that there is a poop bucket full of supplies in classrooms, and panic rooms in hospitals in America in case such an unfortunate event were to happen? Well, there can be many reasons which motivate an individual to reach the point of such violent actions. Reasons include mental illness, bullying, revenge, racial prejudices and so on.

Some may be influenced from shooting video games, or shoot an innocent person because of their beliefs. These mentally sick individuals who kill for these reasons, require loved ones to understand and educate them on why their racist and prejudice beliefs are morally wrong. They may not have loved ones to educate them on this, or they may have loved ones who are also racist and happy to see a coloured man gunned down, as was the case in America which sparked the Black Lives Matter movement.

Many mentally ill people may not comprehend the full depth of their actions on an innocent human life, because they do not see their victim as a human of equal value. They lack the ability to consciously empathize with their victims prior to turning their hateful thoughts into deadly action. They may be influenced from fictitious, racist forums, or the media's portrayal of a certain faith group, such as with Muslims being made out to be terrorists. Meanwhile in reality, real Muslims know that suicide is haram (not allowed) in the Islamic faith, and condemn the actions of those imposter Muslims who kill themselves and innocent people. The lack of understanding of a community can cause hatred. If people take the time to speak to members of the community they have hate for, often they will find that those same people are warm and welcoming, and they had a completely wrong impression of them. This small amount of good shown towards them from the community they once hated, can help prevent the future killing of innocent lives.

Bullying is another reason which can lead to a person picking up their father's assault rifle, going to school one day, and taking out their vengeance on students and teachers whom they felt were the cause of stress in their lives. Often times, bullies are bullies because they find it fun to harass and abuse another student who is physically smaller than themselves. They were likely raised without good morals at home towards their fellow human, so they do not see anything wrong with beating up another student and stealing their lunch money. Years of constantly picking on a nerdy kid and calling them names, or a group of kids spreading a rumor about one poor student, can take a serious toll on a person's mental health. The bully or bullies are having fun at their victim's expense, and do not realize what the victim is feeling or going through as a result of their actions. Weeks or years go by, then one day there is a mass shooting and everyone is wondering why again this is happening. Flowers will envelop the school, and concerned parents will target gun ownership laws, instead of teaching children to not target and bully innocent pupils at school.

I am not saying that people who have experienced being bullied have the right to kill their fellow students. However, if they were not bullied in the first place, they would not have been mentally pressured into thinking that killing was their only option. They wanted to live in peace without their bullies attacking them constantly. Bullies often grow up to become adults with big egos, who talk aggressively and loudly to get their point across and some become influencers. They struggle to think considerately of others, and use their strength to take advantage of physically weaker individuals. A bully may act on his impulsive emotions, and be controlled by his lustful desires and power-hungry nature. He may attack an individual, then accuse his victim of being too emotional when the victim snaps and retaliates in a fierce manner.

What we need to realize is that people who shoot up schools were often bullied by emotional, yet tough guys, to the point where the person bullied reached their breaking point. Due to being skinny and weak, they can get beat up and bullied by bigger guys or a group of people. Then they go literally insane, and lose it after holding in their anger caused by people who bullied them. That is my theory on how and why some of these "psycho" weak guys go shooting up schools.

Unfortunately, lawmakers and school officials often take action in a reactive way, after the occurrence of a deadly event. Rarely are there proactive measures, such as developing severe penalties for bullying in schools. When we consider the circumstances, preventing bullying in schools can save lives. When a society allows bullies to impose on the rights of others, and the victim cannot defend themselves, it creates a society of people with mental illness. When these children reach adulthood, they may shoot one another over a parking spot. If a society wishes to stop a growing, violent norm that is stressful to live with, policies must be implemented to deter and punish bullies in schools. Otherwise, bullies will become increasingly aggressive and violent in adulthood, taking advantage of many people they interact with.

9/11 created tighter security in airports. Covid-19 created better hygienic standards worldwide and tested the occupancy limits of hospitals. Few countries proactively prepare for events such as rare natural disasters, plagues, and the lifestyle and housing needs of a growing community. All which can lead to stressful situations, which could have been avoided with proper planning and implementation. We need to influence our communities to respect and understand each other if we want to significantly reduce the number of school shootings in America. There are countries where people are so honest, that you can leave your laptop in a café, and it will still be there hours later when you return. In some of these societies, people are taught from a young age that stealing, bullying and slander are all wrong.[14]

In order for a society to function optimally, the society as a whole, needs to share the same ideology of what is morally acceptable towards fellow members of their community. If half of the population supports gun ownership and the other half does not, this can create tension and division, which can lead to violence and inefficiencies. When a society is mixed with different races and religions, as many countries are, it is of utmost importance to educate your kids about tolerance, respect and understanding. We may not all share the same views on religion, LGBTQ and gun laws. But if we show respect and tolerance, we can learn to get along harmoniously, without any animosity towards another human being due to a lack of understanding. Difference in beliefs can be a beautiful thing which we can learn from, and take advantage of different points of views for a more progressive society.

There are neighbourhoods in the Caribbean where there can be a church, temple and a mosque all on the same street, surrounded by houses filled with people of each respective different faith. The members of these communities respect each other, and many even attend each other's religious services, without necessarily believing in the same faith. The point is, tolerance, mutual respect and understanding go a long way to promote a peaceful society. We cannot shove our beliefs on others if we want people to respect us. Forcing new LGBTQ policies or religious beliefs on a society can cause more division and conflict. Instead, we must be fair, and equally show respect and support for members of all beliefs living in a society. These seemingly insignificant habits of a nation as a whole, can lead to a much more peaceful and less stressful country to live in.

If I were to suggest to the education board in certain developed countries, that it would be beneficial to implement a mandatory "Ethics" class in public schools, the school board may laugh at the idea and advise me not to waste their time. They would not see such a fundamental class fitting or necessary for a child's development. Later, when those children become adults and violently fight over a limited-edition Christmas toy in a store; everyone wonders how a person can behave in such a manner, as though their parents did not teach them better when they were younger.[15]

The reality is many developed first world nations have ultra-high living and housing costs. To bare these expenses, both parents are typically forced to work full-time, often with overtime, and live further and further away from their places of employment. This limits the allocated time they spend with their children, as well as hampers the amount of energy and patience needed to properly teach and raise a child. Furthermore, many parents lack these fundamental moral values themselves, so they would often teach their children that stealing and bullying is okay to some degree while trying to justify it. This is where the problems start in a society, which escalates when children become adults themselves with a lack of proper ethical teachings.

On the other hand, there are places in Asia where students must take a multi-year class on ethics and how to contribute as a respectful member of society. There are also ads on the radio serving as reminders for things such as not to delay leaving your parking space if you see someone waiting for it. As well, to give up your seat on public transit for a pregnant, disabled or elderly person. These character traits which should come as common sense courtesy, are unfortunately overshadowed by selfish behaviour in many nations where children are raised by social media. Babies grow up staring at a tablet screen, while their parents are busy juggling laundry and preparing dinner.

The nations that have ethics being taught in schools, also have among the lowest gun violence rates in the world.[16] Japan has long been rated as one of the safest, high-income countries in the world. When leaving a public event area, Japanese people will clean the area and will not leave any garbage behind. They will line up orderly waiting for public transit at a train or bus station. Then, they will not talk loudly or have phone conversations on board which may disturb other passengers. When a community is taught to respect others, they will consider the impact that their actions have on another person. They will not break public property to make a social media video for likes. They will not prank others by taking other people's property, or causing people to jump out of fear for an online video challenge. It has happened before where a person has harassed another person, only to be shot in what they initially thought would be a funny prank.[17] Selfish people are controlled by their greed and the possibility of monetary gain, social media popularity or authoritative power. They act thoughtlessly of others who they hurt in their progress to what they define as success. This causes unjustified stress on innocent people, which can lead to anger against the one who caused them undue harm.

At times, the perpetrators may use violence or threats to control you, rape you or steal your money, and prevent you from going to the police if you do not have confidence in the legal system. Furthermore, you may lack the resources to handle the problem on your own without the risk of getting yourself in trouble. You may also fear retaliation if you report your oppressor to the police. Some people take advantage of relatives whose trust they have gained, or family members whom they think would not take any course of justice against their evil actions. Many women are raped by close relatives before they even hit puberty without their parents ever knowing. Children lack the physical strength to fight back, and are often innocent and too naive of the situation before it happens.

People with big houses and pickup trucks can also cause harm to others who do not expect it. A person should think carefully before they mess with someone who has the resources and capabilities of ramming a pickup truck through their business. People may not realize that the person whom they take advantage of, has the ability to kidnap them, and make them disappear in the concrete floor of their basement. It is something that can happen. Therefore, do not take advantage of innocent people in life, and you will not have the stress of having your victims retaliate against you or your family in future. Similarly, you must choose your battles wisely when deciding what to do if someone in power harms you. When possible, protect yourself from those people who prey on the innocent.[18]

In life, someone may scratch your new BMW out of jealousy, or unintentionally crash into your parked car, and drive off without leaving any way for you to contact or find them. There are many different types of people in this world, and most people have diseases in their hearts, such as envy, pride and greed. These are negative traits that people will often be offended of being associated with, even if they inhibit these characteristics. Many will intentionally harm innocent people, spread rumors about a person, and then be upset when they are called a liar, then use more lies to defend themselves.

Arguing with certain ignorant and dishonest people will often cause you greater stress and anxiety. Therefore, we must determine if the long-term possible outcome is worth the time, energy, money and stress involved in battling them. If arguing to prove your point will not lead to any fruitful long-term results which benefit you, then it would be best to just let them be, rather than argue for the sake of arguing if it will not change anything.

Dishonest people will slander the names of others, or otherwise verbally hurt others because they think it is fun. People observing may also laugh at the situation finding it funny. Though in reality, it is painful and mentally harmful to the victim. But most people are too selfish, and only want to enjoy a brief moment of laughter and fun at the expense of the victim's dignity. This can cause the victim to feel isolated and depressed. Sometimes, when you are being bullied by a group of individuals, you may try to speak up and stand up for yourself. However, whether it be your family, co-workers or even a social group at your place of worship, the group bullying you may try to gaslight you into thinking that you are the problem. In this scenario, save messages, conversations, emails and other evidence of the bullying. Compile proof of all false accusations and otherwise untrue portrayal of your character. Then confront them with the facts and evidence, proving that they are wrong. Then defend yourself with the truth by assertively speaking out against them. Advise them that if they persist and do not rectify the situation, you will file a police report and take them to court. Let them know that you are not a wimpy helpless toy to be taken advantage of. This may cause them to then respect you, or hate you more. Either way, this will likely stop the bullying, because even if they do not fear you, they may fear the repercussions of facing you in court. Even if you just threaten to take them to court without actually doing so. Moving forward, keep your life private from these individuals and do not let them know about your personal situation or goals in life. Do not feed them information to use against you.

When you are dealing with an individual, or a group of people who are trying to use lies to frame you, confront them through text on exactly what they are doing. For example, if someone physically harms you, and then sends you a message saying something untrue such as:

"I hope you do not steal my car wheels because of this, like you did with my sister's car."

Immediately reply with the actual facts, clarifying the truth of their motives and actions such as follows:

"You and I fully know that I did not ever steal anyone's wheels including your sister's wheels. You assaulted me, and now are sending me an untrue message trying to manipulate the facts with your lies and deceit so that you can falsify a police report. This shows how dishonest and dangerous you are. Are you not the one who stole your associate's car wheels the night before I helped you when you were moving, and then he called you about it the next day? Should I ask the police to obtain your call log history from your mobile service provider to confirm this, as well as report how you assaulted and threatened me?"

Include any factual criminal behaviour that they are involved in with your messages, and try to obtain evidence you can use to prove these facts. Be cautious around violent people when doing this, so that you do not put yourself and your family's safety at risk. Then file a police report regarding the entire situation, including all of the illegal activity that they are involved in.

Some people will do you wrong for their own gain or benefit, then tell you that it was what you wanted when you confront them about it. For example, your relative or parent may take thousands of dollars from you, use it for their mortgage or buying a new car, then tell you that you wanted to live in that house, or you wanted them to have a nice car for themselves. Assertively tell them that you did NOT want those things, and that they only did it for their own benefit. Tell them what you wanted to clarify if it helps, such as follows.

"I wanted to buy my own house for my future, not have you use my money to pay for your own mortgage which does not benefit me"

"I wanted a chocolate cake for my birthday, not vanilla because your favourite kid does not like chocolate, and whatever they want in life, I must make sacrifices to accommodate."

"I wanted to buy an Integra coupe, not a broken down old car that you used my money for, while pocketing the rest."

"I wanted to study living away from home the way you paid for my older sister to. I did not wish to stay at home and have you cuss and beat me daily, while giving me endless house chores to do, so that I had no time to study."

"I wanted to marry Andrew, not have you force me to marry Jacob because you do business with his family."

Firmly clarify that you did not agree to them using you the way they did, nor making decisions on your behalf which affected your life. Tell them that you do not need them to do such things for you, with your money, time, life or energy. If they promised their friend that you will marry their son, that is not your problem. Tell them you have the right to marry whom you choose, and let them explain to their friend that you will not agree. Distance yourself from the situation, yelling at them within reason if you must.

Do not be afraid to stand up for yourself in a group. It may be with people that you once considered close friends or relatives. Then one day, your mother or someone in the group started a rumor about you, and turned everyone in the group against you. From then on, they all may have treated you badly. People are generally illogical and believe the first bad thing they hear about someone else. Especially if it is from someone such as your mother, because what mother would lie about their own child and make their child look bad, right? Well, it happens, as not all mothers are loving, fair and righteous.

When the rumor first begins, immediately tell everyone that it is a lie about you and tell them the truth. Tell them details as to any previous problems you may have had with this person who started the rumor, and other manipulative things that they have done. Explain the truth in detail so that people know the full situation, and understand why the person may have started a rumor about you. Provide evidence to the group if you can, such as text messages you have between you and the person that started the rumor. It can be a hassle to go through all of this, but in the long run, this can save you many years of stress when seeing these people. If you leave it too long before you try and clear your name, many will not believe you, and you may cause a rumor to turn into people increasingly believing it to be the truth, even though it is not true. When people understand your side and see that you are right from the start, they might help you and back you up.

Chapter 2: Protect Yourself

The best way to deal with traumatic experiences caused by people is to prevent the trauma from taking place. This will require retraining your thinking of how you interact and deal with people on a daily basis. It will be challenging to adopt, especially for soft-hearted, people-pleasing individuals. But you will need to gather your courage and stand up for yourself to prevent people from taking advantage of you. Defending yourself initially against someone trampling over your rights will likely prevent dealing with much more stress later on. Perhaps you have people in your life who constantly ask you to "borrow" money which they may not intend to repay. You may know people who constantly use you for favours or otherwise take advantage of you. You must learn to stand up for yourself with these people, and deny their requests with a firm and assertive "No."

Saying "No" is not selfish. It is a means of protecting yourself from people's ill desire to take advantage of you. It is a way to protect your peace and maintain your place in this world that you strived to achieve. By constantly giving into people's requests for your money, possessions, time, energy or other resources, you are actually training these people to know that you are a pushover. They will view you as a weak and easily manipulated individual, who they can take advantage of and use as they wish, without any repercussions.

Beware of people who deceivingly play nice to get what they want from you such as your wealth. Once they get what they want from you, they will quickly have the upper hand and begin treating you poorly, while speaking condescendingly to you. Later, if they ever do return your wealth, they will act as though they are doing you a favour by returning what was rightfully yours. It tells a lot about a person's character when they ask you for money. A decent, honest and considerate person would not burden another person, unless it is of dire need. People need to learn to be responsible and live within their means. Do not let their problem become your problem. Interrogate them as to why they need to borrow your money, and ask them why they did not plan ahead for the situation so they understand how irresponsible they are. Rudely ask them why they spent their money on luxury bags and concerts instead of saving in case their car needed to be fixed later. Let them feel guilty and embarrassed. Make them understand that it is not so easy to simply ask you for money whenever they want it, in order to take the burden off of themselves and put it on you. Be bold and let people know you are not so easy. However, if they are poor and in dire need, and you can help them, then use your discretion and help them in charity. You may be greatly improving their life, and you may receive back more than what you gave in some other way.

When something good happens in your life and you just cannot wait to tell someone about it, STOP! Do not mention it to anyone, have your favourite dessert or treat yourself to celebrate and enjoy it quietly. Remember, people are jealous and envious creatures. There of course are exceptions, such as if you are starting a business and need to ask your uncle for advice, as he may have experience in the matter. As well, you should always share big movements in your life with your partner in order to maintain open communication and trust.

Do not flash your wealth. Do not ever reveal your true wealth, income, your sex life, your blessings, your bad character traits or who your best friends are to people. Keep your private personal information secret from those who do not need to know. When possible, keep your valuable possessions private and hidden from the public, friends and relatives. It is better to be modest and downplay your game, rather than live extravagantly trying to show off. Do not broadcast on social media your flashy new car, your son's sports achievements or daughter's new job or house purchase. Most people will not be genuinely happy for you and your family's achievements. Even if people like your posts and comment "Congratulations," in reality most will be jealous and envy you, wishing for misfortune to strike you. If you want to live a peaceful life, be rich not famous. This way you can enjoy your blessings, without worrying of jealous people wishing to bring you down when they have the chance. It may also be beneficial to have only a few close and trusted people following you on social media.

When you make friends in life through different avenues such as university, a local book club, volunteering at your local religious place of worship, or through social media, do not mix your friends. You may think you can trust everyone and think that everyone is friendly and nice, so it would be fun to have one big group of friends. However, do not be naive to the fact that people are selfish, and will happily screw you over for their benefit. You do not own people, not your kids, not your social group with over two hundred people that you created, not anyone. They do not care that they all know each other through you. Do not expect loyalty in people. As well, do not have too high expectations of people in this world.

This world can be beautiful, forming good relationships with people you meet; or it can be ugly, seeing the evil within people on a daily basis. Do not have expectations of a friendship to last a lifetime when you meet someone new for the first time. Avoid telling people of your salary, what vehicle you drive and where you live. Avoid letting friends you are not close with know your address, or they may vandalize your property or rob you out of jealousy or hate if the opportunity arises. Most people have no right to know your assets and personal information. Do not trust people easily at all in life. Trust must be earned, and not something you give out without learning what the person stands for in their core beliefs.

Friends can also be a benefit in your life. When socializing, you will likely learn many new things about life which you did not know. Everyone knows something, and no one knows everything. We all come from different walks of life, and have different educational backgrounds and upbringing. You can learn about a field you did not study in by observing and listening to others in this field. You may learn of a new show which you might like from a friend, or discover a new pizza restaurant to try. When interacting with others who have different opinion from your own, they can help you take a fresh look at things when you are dealing with a problem or conflict. Do not entirely cut off everyone just because they have a few negative traits. Be aware of what their personality, values and habits are, so that you can better deal with them in a manner that does not abuse your friendship. However, if it is a bad trait such as lying, which has impacted the friendship significantly, then it is best to block that person out of your life.

Lying is a trait which evil people use to conceal their faults, steal, deceive, as well as turn others against another individual. Do not ever trust a person who is a compulsive liar. Stay far away from them and protect your connections from them as well. Most people can be easily influenced by others, even without any proof. In some Western countries, a woman can say that you yelled at her, hit her or sexually assaulted her, and everyone from your own friends, the police and the courts will believe her, simply because she says it happened even though it did not. She will call her friends and family, as well as your own friends and family, while she fake cries to them in a soft desperate voice, stating lies about you to manipulate them into believing her and hating you. Then she will file a police report and take you to court, recalling the people she complained to about you as "witnesses." She may also visit these friends and family members to fake cry and complain to them for a more impactful and believable effect. She may send you emails and messages, referencing incidents of abuse which did not take place, to further build credibility to her false allegations and slanderous lies as she misuses the court system. The people who once loved you, will turn against you without questioning or verifying any details of the claims made by her. The only thing they "witnessed" was her speaking lies about you to them, and no one witnessed the actual alleged occurrences of abuse or whatever it may be that she is stating against you. Stay away from these women and do not trust anything they say, even if they tell you that they will lie against someone you dislike to protect you. Eventually, she may use her same lying weaponized tactics against you.

Never connect people trying to fill a void in life with friends for the lack of having a loving family. These dear friends of yours will not have the same adornment for you as you do for them. You are simply a person to talk to and experience fun activities together, with no love, attachment nor commitment. If you become an inconvenience, they will easily let you go without any pain in their hearts; for they already receive love and affection from their actual families, so they do not yearn for attention from you.

Avoid wasting your time being nice and trusting of everyone you consider a friend while connecting them all. You cannot control people nor dictate their lives. In large groups, especially with singles, you can expect behaviour such as backstabbing, people sleeping around with multiple other people in the group, and the occasional argument which they may blame you for. You will face a lot of stress with little reward if you are the leader of the group and a soft-hearted pushover. If you think you can trust everyone and combine your friends together, one dishonest person in your group of friends may screw you over by creating a separate chat group with all of the members from your original chat group except you. Instead of anyone telling you about it, they may fear not being included in the fun group, so they will not show any loyalty to you nor inform you about what is going on.

Many people today would be passive-aggressive with a person and pretend to be their friend to their face, while slandering their name and excluding them behind their back. Many people today lack the comprehension and social maturity to calmly confront a person and discuss any disagreements. They choose to ignore that person, or pretend to be their friend while secretly disliking them. This can be confusing to the person that is treated this way, as they may even consider the other person as a real friend, and still do things for that person. They are eventually left heartbroken when they discover the truth about their friendship, and all the events the other person excluded them from.

If you are in a large friend group, someone in the group can start a disgusting rumor about you. For example, if you were interested in a girl for marriage, and her sister lies by saying that you whispered in her ear. This can prevent you from marrying the girl of your dreams, while you watch her marry a pilot or a doctor instead. If this happens to you in a large, combined group of friends which you created, instead of losing one group of friends, you will be isolated from all your friends that you made in life through different avenues. This can cause you to face torment and loneliness which you do not deserve. Keep your friend groups separate, and perhaps at your engagement ceremony or wedding they will have the privilege of meeting each other. That way, when hormones and jealousy come into play, and one person likes another from your other group of friends, they will be less likely to screw you over since you are already in the process of marriage.

Regardless of whether you wish to get married or not, focus your time, energy and resources on yourself. Be loyal to yourself and trust yourself. Most friends will lie to you to make you feel good about a bad situation. A true friend will be honest and tell you the truth, such as a bad habit you have, even if it hurts you. A true and honest friend will tell you when you have mucus in your nose before your big speech. Fake friends will let you go on stage and laugh at you behind your back, then pat you on the back and tell you that you did a good job afterwards.

When it comes to romance, both men and women can be very deceiving, manipulative and evil, in order to attract and acquire the person whom they desire. They do not care that you were the one to introduce them as acquaintances. They do not care that you knew that person first, and that you already made it clear that you are interested in that person. If a person wants something in life, most are readily inclined to use unethical means to obtain that thing. This holds true with romance, jobs, money, land and other material things. Even many politicians around the world are corrupt and accept money, gifts and favours which they are not intitled to.[19]

Do not think so innocently to believe that just because you would never do such a thing, it means that the majority of people would also never do such an evil act. Lying, cheating and stealing are prevalent in most societies around the globe, and without specific laws in a country, people would be killing other people for their property and raping women in the streets. We must especially be aware of the dangerous thoughts of others in the modern times that we live in; where many churches are closing down, and an increasing amount of the population in certain countries are becoming atheist.[20] When people do not believe in God, nor heaven and hell as reward and punishment for the way they treat others, they have little or no motivation preventing them from taking advantage of others.

When some people discover you are wealthy, they may be drawn to you. Not because of your personality or character, but instead to try and benefit from you or learn your secrets to becoming financially successful. Guard yourself, your business secrets and your wealth from these people. They may refuse to believe that you earned it through hard work. Most people want an easy, fast-track way to gain a lot of money in a short amount of time with little effort. This is especially true in Western society with labour rights, unions, and a lazy mentality of workers. People want high salaries with little work, whereas in many third world developing countries, people are unfortunately not always protected by fair labour laws. In developing countries, people often work hard for a small wage which may barely cover their meals and necessities each month. Developing countries often have manual labour employees who manufacture products, which are sold and consumed by wealthier first world nations. Some may say that this involves child labour or unfair manual labour exploitation. Though many who say this, would still rather purchase products at a relatively low price, and close their eyes ignoring the facts of how or where it was manufactured.

Some people may see an image of a dead baby in a war-torn country and donate a small amount of money to a large charity organization. They then feel good about themselves, as though they are not selfish, and as though they made a big difference towards the cause. However, many large charities have CEOs making six-figure salaries and have very high overhead costs. This means that only a small portion of the donation actually gets used towards helping those in need. Do research on where you donate; sometimes smaller local charities have more of an impact towards the cause. Some people donate to make themselves feel good, or even worse, do it for clout to make their followers and society think that they are generous. Regardless what little good a person does, they may still have much evil in them, so you need to protect yourself. They may be quick to screw you over in a business deal or take advantage of a family member. Should the opportunity arise, many would scam money from an innocent person quickly, if they think that they will not be brought to justice for it. They may snatch money out of your wallet when you go to the washroom, or sell off your belongings which you entrust them with when you go travelling.

Each generation is faced with different ethics and work mentality. Elders in many first world nations were expected to work hard, often in manufacturing jobs, before those jobs became obsolete being replaced by machines and sent overseas. They often purchased things in cash and avoided debt when possible. Newer generations think that it is best to work smart, and if a machine can do a job almost as good as a person, and at a fraction of the cost, then it is best to automate that job. Upcoming generations may feel that investing in crypto currency and becoming an influencer will be a fast-track way to success, then may feel depressed when they lose their life savings or lose their friends.

The way people value and interact with people and money has also changed. Respecting the property of others and not taking what does not belong to you, has become replaced with people borrowing money for most big purchases and financing with loans they do not expect to pay off before they die. Many people live using borrowed money, while living paycheck to paycheck. The majority of people do not save for an unexpected financial crisis, such as if they were to lose their job or have unforeseen medical expenses. They are just a few paychecks away from living on the streets. The reason I am explaining this to you, is so that you can become aware of the mentality of most people. This is vital in order to understand the situation many have put themselves in. They will ask to borrow your money so that you can fund their lavish lifestyle. If their boss gave them a raise, they may use that money to finance a more luxurious car instead of paying off the loan for their existing vehicle. Most people never feel content with what they currently own, and are always wanting more. Therefore, when they see you doing well in life, especially if you are doing better than them, they become envious of you and will try to take from you.

Regardless if it is money or good looks, conceal your wealth and beauty if you wish to live a peaceful life. Many women say they wear fancy clothes and do their makeup for themselves. Yet when they are alone at home they are without makeup and wearing sweatpants. The truth is, we love attention and crave admiration from others. This is a desire especially true for women whom love compliments and attention from guys they are interested in, or find sexually desirable. However, if the man that is complimenting them is unattractive, he may be labelled as a creep as this is unwanted attention for most women. As a woman, it is important to be very honest with yourself.

In some culture and belief systems, women cover their hair and dress modestly when out in public to preserve their beauty and modesty. Some of these women who cover their hair, still dye their hair with colouring because they like the way it makes them look, even though out in public no one will see it. These women are often more devoted to their husbands, and dress sexy at home for only their husband to enjoy their beauty. If the husband is a good provider and an honest man, these relationships usually are more peaceful, with both partners trusting each other with full faithfulness. Most men do not even care if you wear the same dress multiple times. However, you must be honest about your concerns of being judged by other women, and dressing sexy to the night club or dinner out with friends, hoping to gain attention. Once you have this self-awareness, you will be able to differentiate between what YOU want, verses what you do to attract the attention of others. It is perfectly okay to dress down and go out, or not try so hard to impress others.

Focus on keeping healthy both physically and mentally, and keep a good honest character which is a rare quality these days. Keep your weight down and be genuine, instead of gossiping about others and putting people down in an attempt to make yourself look good. An average weight girl in baggy gym clothes, with an honest and sweet personality, is far more attractive than a thin girl wearing barely any clothes and dancing provocatively. Dressing slutty and being promiscuous will attract the f-boys who just want to use your sexy body. They have absolutely no intention to call you the next day in pursuit of a serious relationship, nor support you or your child if you have one. Cover your sexy body if you are an attractive female. This will limit the bad attention from perverted men who lack morals and self-discipline. Keep your friends' circle small and limited to the few who will be there if you need help. Many people are in your life for a fun ride when it is beneficial to them, while they give nothing in return.

Set boundaries when dealing with anyone in life. Whether someone is invading your personal bubble of space around your body, or if they are asking you to do something unreasonable. Verbally and assertively communicate to them when they are nearing your boundaries. If they become physical with you, and if you are strong and capable enough, then become physical with them in self-defence, within reason. Do not be afraid to ask for your rights or say no. You can say no if you are being used. "No, sorry but I cannot help you with that." Saying "No" is not mean or unkind, it means that you are protecting yourself and putting yourself first.

There are a few soft-hearted individuals whom you can be kind and generous with, but with most people in life, you will need to protect yourself from being used. If you have a friend that you constantly drive places, ask them to top up your fuel tank with some petrol now and then, do not feel shy. The more you do things for people, the more you are encouraging them to expect consistently more from you in future. It may reach the point where you feel stressed out doing too much for them, without receiving anything in return. If you finally say "No" one day, they will suddenly hate you and forget all the good you did for them previously. People are selfish and ungrateful by nature. Therefore, in order to avoid feeling stress from them increasingly using you, set boundaries from the start of the relationship.

In life, you may have an employer who pushes your boundaries, such as ordering you to work overtime constantly without pay, or making you work during your lunch breaks and not allowing you to take your entitled vacation days. They may do this without giving you a raise in salary ever, and make you feel guilty if you refuse to do optional duties in your role. For this situation, you can of course look for another job. Alternatively, you can work to rule for your job title. This means, doing only what is expected of you, as per your job description and any contract agreed upon. Take your lunch breaks which you are entitled to. Do not feel guilty for not covering the workload of three people because they decided to layoff two of your co-workers. When you die, your employer will easily replace you, so why kill yourself trying to please them when they do not care about you? Know that you can never please everyone in life, so do what is fair and balance what is best for you and those affected by you, such as in your job.

Do not ask people for permission when you are doing something within your rights. Otherwise, they will look at you as being weak and consider you as their subordinate. They may also refuse your request, even though you are entitled to that which you ask of them. Instead, simply tell them out of respect, "I am taking my lunchbreak at 1 p.m.," instead of asking if you can have your lunchbreak at a certain time. Also, clearly communicate your needs with people in order to avoid any misunderstandings which can turn into stressful situations. If you have an important doctor's appointment on a certain date, ensure that you clearly state the importance of your appointment to your employer. This way, they do not think you merely wish to leave early to go for a coffee date with a friend.

Mental wellbeing can also relate to how you get to use your time. Do not let others use you, by robbing you of valuable minutes of your life to help them when they are moving or need their deck painted. Especially when you do not even like them. Do not let anyone turn you into their slave. Even if they are physically bigger than you, love yourself enough to stand up for yourself. Do not let them intimidate you into doing free manual labour when you should be studying or working. Use your time as you wish to bring yourself happiness and peace. Do not waste your time doing things that take away your peace.

When involved in a dispute, the other party may mention minor mistakes you have unintentionally made in life to point out your imperfections. In such a case, be sure to clearly let them know the bigger, immoral and unjust things which they have intentionally done to you. Do not fear them, and make it clear that you are willing to take legal action against them. If someone asks you to do something that you do not want to do, ask them why they cannot do it themselves. If you feel this is a rude reply and you have respect for them, you may respond with asking them for a favour in return, even if you do not need any assistance. "Sure, I can help you change the cabin filter in your car, but first can you help me tidy up my shed?" Watch how quickly they may respond with suddenly no longer needing your assistance.

When people ask you a question that you do not feel comfortable answering, such as inquiring how much your salary is, you can ask why they want to know. additionally, you may also ask them to tell you how much money they make first. Alternatively, you can tell them that it is a very personal matter, and you cannot share that information. You can even ask them to show you their paycheck and make them realize how uncomfortable it can be when asking very personal questions. This also demonstrates that you are requesting proof of what they are saying by asking to see their paycheck, so they will know that you do not trust their words.

When you make friends or form relationships in life, sometimes you may drift apart. Do not fight for people to be in your life who do not want you. If they do not owe you anything and do not appreciate you, let them go so that you can focus on your future success without them. Invest in things that help make you money and bring you good health and happiness. Do not waste time and money trying to keep up with fake friends who may only be temporary in your life.

When you are an attractive woman, you must be vigilant with who you allow to be close to you. Some guys will lie and tell you that they love you, promising that they will marry you solely to have sex with you. Then they will end things and move on to their next victim after they take your virginity or sleep with you. Whether you are a girl or guy, people will often wrong you when they do not fear harm from you, either physical or otherwise. Therefore, it is important to take precautions in life. Lock your car doors after entering your vehicle. As well, learn self-defence such as martial arts, to better protect yourself from people trying to take advantage of you. If you are a woman and find yourself being attacked by a man, a strong and direct kick to his testicles, may temporarily disable him enough to give you time to escape and find help. Do not miss.

It is unfortunate that places such as Canada, lack sufficient self-defence laws to protect victims from violent criminals.[21] In some instances, criminals may even sue their victims for defending themselves. This contributes to high stress levels and mental health illnesses within victims of violent crimes who were unable to legally defend themselves. These unfortunate, peaceful individuals may become victims of the legal system, being classified as criminals themselves for simply defending their property and loved ones. Defending one's self comes as a natural human instinct as well as among animals. It is a raw biological system in our species to defend and protect ourselves when we are being attacked.[22]

Imagine a scenario where five large males are ramming through the front door of your condo unit. This is an immediate threat to the safety of yourself, as well as anyone else under your guardianship. The criminals may be unknown to you, and they may be willing to use violence against you and your family to get what they want. Do they want to rape your wife? Are they in search of your car keys to steal your Mercedes? You may believe common sense dictates that you should be able to legally defend yourself against an intruder with whatever means necessary. The intruder made the commitment to intentionally break into your private, safe space which you call your home. So, you in turn may think that it is your home, your rules. However, after they made the choice to violate the privacy and safety of your family and yourself, the criminals are still entitled to many rights in certain countries. So much so, that some might argue that criminals have more rights than the victims whom they terrorize.

This can be a very stressful ordeal for the unfortunate and innocent people who are faced with such an experience. Not everyone can afford to replace their belongings once they are stolen. As well, if one of your family members were killed by an intruder, their life will never be replaced, and you will lose them for the rest of your life. In order to reduce mental health issues, decrease violent crime, and bring peace and justice to a society, a country must enable its citizens to legally defend themselves and their property against perpetrators who prey on the innocent. Allow individuals to use justified force to disable their attacker to the point where they are no longer a threat.

Do not force victims to wait and see what will happen next, giving the unlawful and immoral criminal the benefit of the doubt. Do not force people to look on and hope that their attacker will not do any worse to them than they already have. If you were to simply punch your attacker once in their arm, and ask them politely to stop, they might become enraged and kill you as a response. People need the right to protect themselves in order to feel safe in the country that they want to call home. The law must be defined in clear terms to state what constitutes as "reasonable" force, while providing numerous specific examples of criminal behaviour and acceptable victim responses.

The alternative natural response would be to run away from the danger and hide. However, when faced with an intruder or attacker, this is not very effective at protecting your family and property. If you have an issue with the laws in the land where you live, contact your regional government representative, and start a petition in order to change the laws to promote common sense and a peaceful community.

You may also take legal steps forward as a means of preventing yourself from being put in such a situation as a home invasion, where you can be penalized for protecting yourself or your loved ones. If your region of residence allows it, put barb wire up on your fences and install bars on your windows. Use high-definition night capable cameras around your home, which alert your phone to any disturbances at your residence.

Drive a vehicle capable of protecting you, such as one that utilizes high strength steel to protect the passenger compartment in case of a serious collision. Use tracking devices on your vehicles to locate them in case they are stolen. One major city in a first world country faced over eight thousand cases of vehicle theft in one year alone! There are incidents where people would track their stolen vehicles and report the location to the police. The police would then advise the victims not to go and retrieve their vehicle themselves over safety concerns.[23] If the police are occupied and unable to respond in a timely manner, the victim would need to contact their insurance company and deal with the stress of trying to buy another vehicle. This occurred during times of inflated market prices, due to pandemic chip shortages and dealer markups for high demand vehicles.

It is unfortunate that innocent people often bare the losses caused by criminals due to insufficient preventative laws. We must realize this might be the society we live in. If you were to confront the person or group of people who stole your vehicle, they may become violent with you. If you were to physically harm them while defending yourself, you may face legal ramifications. So, we need to protect and defend ourselves as best as we can, without violating any laws which may put us in a situation of dealing with more loss and stress as a result of any repercussions. We do not live in an ideal world, so we must consider a variety of possible outcomes for conflict scenarios. This way, we can then decide upon our actions when dealing with people. In life, do not assume things about others without solid proof. Also, do not assume that others know your innocent intentions without you clearly explaining the reasons for your actions. Consider how law enforcement, the general public, news outlets and courts will view your actions when deciding how best to handle interactions with people.

I can recall numerous times in my life when guys I just met would comment in my presence, telling me their sexual desires of a particular woman they may have just met. They would mention the things they would try and do with her whilst she was out of listening distance. These men would talk to me as though I was just one of the guys like many other men, not knowing my values were different and I practice celibacy by choice. I would have little choice but to do an awkward fake laugh and remove myself from the situation; or warn the girl of the particular man's intentions, if it were a girl that I knew would not wrongfully accuse me of being the liar. Which is another issue entirely as to why so many of us are afraid to caution or correct someone. The person you are trying to help may accuse you of being jealous, ingenuine or having evil alternative motives, when you are simply trying to be a good friend. Often, people will become scared of you or a group of people, if they do not know and understand you. Until they learn to know you and witness the values that you represent, they may not care to listen to what you say in your defence, and they may just go on hating you.

We need to understand how people operate, and the motives behind why they do the things they do, which hurt innocent people. Some people are driven by hatred, jealousy, greed or lack of understanding. We must acknowledge that no society is perfect. Many times, innocent people may be taken advantage of, especially if they cannot legally defend themselves. For decades, a small fraction of racist police officers in America have gotten away with killing innocent Black men.[24] This was especially common before the popularity of cell phone cameras. We do not need to go back very far in history to see that America was built off the backs of Black slaves,[25] on land that was violently taken from Native Americans.[26] Even within the last few generations, places in North America would not allow women to open a bank account without their husband's permission,[27] and violence was an acceptable means of discipline.[28] Furthermore, when African Americans were free in the US, they were still not given the same rights as their White counterparts for gun ownership and land rights privileges to buy property in certain neighborhoods.[29]

No person should be regarded as superior solely based on their skin colour, gender or other attribute given to them at birth. The racism in the US has created a generational wealth gap of which the effects can still be seen today. Where White people were privileged to work, while Black people were used as slaves to make White people become wealthier. The financial inequality continued after the end of slavery, as White people were able to invest in land and housing, which is regarded as one of the most secure assets possible.

Since property typically always appreciates in value long-term, the Black people who did not have any significant savings coming out of slavery were left behind in this rat race. When a young Black person would finally be able to get a job, they would often be expected to help their families and not be able to save much to invest in purchasing property. This wealth inequality cycle continues over generations. The ones with property save on rent and make money through house appreciation, while those without property continue to pay someone else's mortgage through rental payments. This is an injustice and can cause generational stress, both financially and mentally, which can in turn lead to physical health issues.

The far reaches of one's injustice on another can cause rippling effects that last a lifetime on their victims, which the perpetrator often would not realize. In a few cases in history the impact of this injustice is acknowledged. However, even fewer times are there any steps taken to right the wrongs caused. Therefore, although it may be fair to receive compensation from our oppressors, we should not be expecting the British Royal Family to compensate the generations of slaves born into poor economic status due to their actions.

As well, you should not expect to always be compensated when you are wronged by someone in life. Someone could slander your name at the office, which prevents you from receiving a promotion you deserved. This is a hard reality for some to accept, but we can look at our own situations compared to past events in slavery, as well as modern oppression such as people building illegal settlements on the land of others.[30] As horrible as your situation is, there likely are millions suffering worse than yourself, such as not having clean drinking water or daily meals to sustain themselves. This world is a torment for some, but you must try to make the best out of the situations you face in life.

You may work hard and try to build your dreams, buy your brand-new dream car, and then when it is only three years old someone crashes into it, writing it off. Some people say "Well, that's why you have insurance!" Yet, after depreciation, your $60,000 car may have depreciated to $35,000, and that is all the insurance company will pay you back. So, you are then left having to put in the additional $25,000 loss for someone else's fault in order to replace your car with another brand-new comparable car. That would be $25,000 worth of working hours that you need to repeat at your job and save after living expenses, which can equate to years of your life. Instead, you could have been saving and using that money to go towards things such as paying for your child's university education. Alternatively, you may end up buying someone else's poorly maintained, problematic car, and be stuck with the added stress of fixing and repairing a vehicle that was not as well taken care of as your own.

To demonstrate the long-term effects that a person's actions may have on another individual, I will tell you a true story of a man I know. His parents were physically abusive with him from his childhood onwards, until he moved out of the stressful environment and rented a basement to live in. His father would take money from him since he was seven years old. This individual was the one-in-a-million kid that was actually saving his money since he was very young, as he knew what he wanted in life and was very mature for his age. When the kid grew into an adult and reached the age of twenty-one, he was ready to move to another country and buy a house there paying in cash without needing a mortgage. He had already obtained his visa, and secured a real estate agent and job offer at his intended destination. However, his father, who had anger management issues, also had much of this young man's money. As if that were not bad enough, this twenty-one-year-old trusted his aunt, who advised him to let her convert the remainder of his life savings into the other country's currency so that he could move. She told him that she gets a better exchange rate due to her employment through the bank. He proceeded in giving her his money to exchange when he would have gotten a good value for the currency exchange rate. She refused to sign anything at the time, and out of fear of getting abused by his parents, he could not raise his voice or become more assertive about insisting on her signing or returning his money. As the weeks turned into months, he had to go to his aunt's house to pretend to be happy spending time there, while gently reminding her about his money that he needed to move. She continually brushed him off until a few more months passed, and he got word that she had run away from her husband with a much older man, who left his wife and kids for her. She had pre-packed boxes of her belongings, then on a carefully planned night she called the emergency distress number, 9-1-1, and lied to the authorities stating that her husband was trying to kill her that night. The police arrested her husband, and she had her cousin pick her up and load up the boxes with her belongings.

When the young man was able to contact her, he confronted her about his life savings she took from him. She again brushed him off and told him that she does not have to give him back his money. She advised him if he continues asking her for it, she will lie to the police and tell them that he was trying to kill her. She would be able to bruise herself and rip her clothing to make it look legitimate, and the way the legal system worked in Canada, the country that this happened in, he would be at high risk of being framed for things he did not do. He was up to date with relevant events in society to know that he would have trouble pursuing her for the money she took from him, in addition to the money his father had of his. Life is tough when you do not have parents on your side. Life can be even more difficult when your parents abuse you, take your money and slander your name, leaving you without anyone to turn to for help.

This young man was unable to buy his house at a young age and start his life as he planned. By now, perhaps he would have multiple rental properties in his name and be living very comfortably. Instead, he was forced to use his salary towards renting a small basement, when he should have been living rent-free and putting his salary towards investment properties. A strong argument can be made that his family and relatives prevented him from living his dreams, getting married and having a family of his own. He is now in his thirties, still a virgin and unmarried, while his relatives enjoy their lives without a care for him.

The people who harm us and steal money specifically, often do not do so out of desperation, but instead out of pure greed and evil within them. For a few unfortunate souls, even your own parents and relatives will rob you. Then they will wish you were dead so they do not have to deal with you asking them for your money back. These lying, cheating and stealing relatives have a psychopathic-killer mindset, and should be in jail for life. Though unfortunately, the ones they wrong often do not have the backing and support to defend themselves. From childhood to adulthood, some people are advantageous bullies. This is why I advise you to protect yourselves from being hurt and taken advantage of, especially if you do not have a good social support network who can assist you in times of need.

It is helpful to have good friends in your network in law enforcement, legal aid, healthcare, and a good mechanic to name a few. Because people are animals, and without laws and worry of social reputation, many would be stealing, killing and raping if they felt they would not face repercussions. Just like soldiers who invade other countries and rape the local women while killing their male relatives.[31] For many, this is raw human nature without societal rules preventing people from acting on their impulses.

Chapter 3: Government, Economics and Stress from Society

Unfortunately, outdated or unrealistic government regulations often create a stressful environment for people in their daily lives. Hardships created from the cost of living are a primary concern for many. Certain taxes in some developed regions of the world were created during times of war when it was deemed necessary.[32] These wars have since ended, yet the government continues to charge its citizens certain taxes and has significantly increased taxes over time.[33] It is easy for governments to see the financial benefit taxes produce for themselves and the nation. Unfortunately, some governments treat taxpayer dollars as an unlimited flowing money jar, which they can use however they wish within regulatory constraints.[34] One government may begin a multimillion-dollar project in health care, energy or transportation such as building an underground transit system; only to have it scrapped half-way through after four years, when the new government in charge decides to invest taxpayer dollars into an above ground transit system instead.[35]

Many members of parliament were born into privileged, wealthy homes, and never experienced living through poverty. Consequently, when they are making decisions which affect the working class, they cannot comprehend how their decisions may negatively impact the daily lives of the poor or lower-middle class. Many whom are considered middle class, do not qualify for low-income rebates and incentives, yet do not make enough to live comfortably. Whereas, in poorer nations which may be referred to by some as backwards countries, the rulers often arise from being raised in poor ghettos or villages, with upwards of eight people living in a small wooden house resembling a shack. This disparity in upbringing, can be prominently realized when we compare the utilizing of taxpayer dollars by each country. Through efficiency, poorer countries can achieve more than wasteful wealthy nations.[36] Unfortunately, some wealthy nations continue to tax their citizens heavily,[37] but do not invest in beneficial, long-term development for the country.[38]

In order to build a healthy and harmonious community, we need to relate to the values of the people, and not make things financially difficult for people to live. People are increasingly tired, drained and stressed out. They are trying their best and working hard, yet feel they can barely get by. When irresponsible government policies create increased housing and rent prices, increased traffic congestion and decreased free public services such as health care; this can create a toxic and mentally unfriendly environment to live, work and play in. This is first world poverty. Many couples have decided not to have children due to the increased living costs of society today, which past generations never suffered through. People are moving two to three hours away from their place of employment, because their salary does not cover the basic costs of housing in the same city they work in.[39] Even when moving to the outskirts of a metropolitan city such as Toronto, Vancouver, Tokyo, Hong Kong or New York City, it is harder for the majority of people to survive than ever before, primarily in relation to the cost of housing.

In the year 1990, a high school educated man could get a job working in a factory or driving a taxi in Toronto, while his wife could stay home with their three young children. They could purchase a four-bedroom, three-washroom, two-car garage landed house for around $200,000. Fast forward twenty years, coming out of a recession in the year 2010, and that same house would cost approximately $400,000. That averages to a $10,000 increase per year (excluding interest costs), which many may consider to be a reasonable rate of inflation for a home. However, twelve years later, that same house would be worth close to $1.6 million, or about four times its value previously.

Yet, the average salary did not increase significantly enough to keep up with the ever-increasing house prices of an interest-based society. Those who were fortunate enough to get into the housing market early on in the GTA (Greater Toronto Area), were able to benefit some years from over $100,000 price increases in a single year, simply by doing nothing other than owning a house. This is much more than the vast majority of people can save in a year, including dual-income professional couples with no children. This has caused a disparity between people of the GTA as the haves, and the have-nots, with the majority of Generation Z residents giving up on ever owning a house in Toronto.[40]

Often times, people stay in a place or situation they are in because they cannot imagine a better life being achievable for themselves. They stay because they happened to be born in a certain country, and established some friendship connections and know all the good food places nearby. They stay because they are afraid of taking a leap forward to another land, and are afraid of leaving their family and loved ones behind. Lastly, many fear the financial risk of leaving their abusive marriage or crappy job to explore their options in the world.

It is a shame when a person is educated in the country they were born in, yet cannot afford to stay and live there. It is a shame when governments waste taxpayer dollars and make poor long-term decisions, which cause future generations to struggle with housing affordability. It is a shame when it becomes acceptable for governments to have an excessively high budget deficit, which creates further problems for future governments to clean up. It is a damn shame.

Privileged, spoiled, immature, financially-illiterate bratty mentality, making huge decisions that impact a nation long-term, but they only see the small short-term gain in things. There was an instance where the government of a particular country spent approximately $1.5 billion of taxpayer money to build a toll highway. Initially, this seems like a great idea, as it can generate income and benefit many future generations. However, instead of maintaining control of such a valuable asset, the toll highway was leased to a private company for ninety-nine years, at the low price of only $3.1 billion.[41] Twenty years later, the toll highway was valued at an estimated $30 billion minimum.[42]

This causes the government, through their own actions, to miss out on almost a century's worth of toll revenue, which would have been able to support jobs, infrastructure, and allow citizens to be less burdened by taxes. This government gave up control over toll revenue and price increases. Within this same first world country, a majority stake of a vital electric utility company was sold to private investors.[43] This is an essential service for residents, which also generates revenue. For long-term strategic benefit, governments must prevent companies who have a monopoly in the market, from overcharging consumers and burdening the residents who utilize these services. Selling a majority stake in such a valuable asset, provides short-term gain at the expense of lost future revenue and control. Essential services such as electricity, should be owned and regulated solely by the government if possible. Alternatively, a private company may build the infrastructure and manage the company, provided that regulations are in place to prevent massive price hikes and service interruptions to consumers. A lesson many governments have yet to learn.

Many were born and educated in Canada and love their country, but due to the increased cost of living and housing, many find it unaffordable to stay. Vancouver and Toronto have been named two of the top ten most expensive cities in the world to live in, and this is not something to be proud of.[44] A shortage of homes for people to live in, coupled with prolonged low interest rates, all contributed to a surge in the cost of homes for citizens who want to buy.[45] Not to mention, policies which allowed foreign non-national buyers, to purchase houses with no minimum purchase price. Due to increased demand from the work from home trend, even smaller towns hours outside of the main cities have become unaffordable for the Canadian dream of home ownership. Sadly, the situation is not much better in several big cities across the globe, where many are forced to choose between eating healthy food or paying rent. To prevent this, implementing basic measures such as a minimum purchase price for foreign home buyers would help preserve housing affordability for local citizens.

To combat the cost of living, some governments act by simply increasing the minimum wage, instead of reducing government salaries and wasteful spending to then reduce taxes. Drastically raising the minimum wage causes an ongoing cycle of more inflation. Prices at restaurants and grocery stores will increase, as store owners must increase prices to keep up with the increased salaries of their employees. Then the government may raise the minimum wage again, which will cause more inflation once again. Often, those working in minimum wage jobs such as fast-food or grocery stores, are semi-retired, students or those in households where they are not the primary source of income for their families.

A more strategic approach would be to target minimum wage salaries against specific working roles in different industries. This way, an entry level mechanic can be making more than a person working part-time in a fast-food establishment; thus, choosing to build their profession in the automotive industry, instead of flipping burgers for life. It will give people an incentive to do better for themselves. As well, maximum pricing caps for certain essential products such as fresh produce should be implemented, to prevent the monopoly of certain companies unnecessarily overcharging consumers for basic goods.

We must see the trends in industries, such as petrol-powered vehicles being phased out by governments and being replaced with fully-electric vehicles. In the coming years from now, people will realize the unexpected shortcomings and costs associated with having a fully-electric vehicle society.[46] They may then revert back to offering some petrol-powered vehicles for sale again, alongside electric ones. Eventually, hydrogen-powered vehicles will become recognized and approved for use by each respective governing body. However, the fully-electric phase has only just begun to gain mass popularity. Most cannot use their intellect to foresee the trends in order to prepare and adapt. Power grids and infrastructure may need to be upgraded,[47] and more ethical and plentiful mining of raw minerals for batteries will need to be found.[48] Eventually, many may find themselves late for meetings, because they were unable to find an available electric charging station during a busy holiday weekend. This is why foresight is important to avoid applying undue stress on a society.

As the baby boomer population is aging and dying off, we need new incentives for young people to join in professions which baby boomers are retiring from. As an example, skilled trades are a great way to establish a high-paying profession, without spending the time and high investment cost in a typical university degree program. As new technologies will replace millions of jobs in the very near future, it is important to see the trends in society, and prepare to make money and survive so that you can enjoy a peaceful life.[49]

Making money is especially important if you are a man with a family to take care of. In some places, it is difficult to be a man. With high taxes and a high cost of living, an average working man cannot afford a house. As well, there may be laws which protect criminals, preventing you from defending your wife and daughter. You need family backing, money and a big physique to fully protect yourself from people taking advantage of you. If you have a significant portion of any of these three things, you can still reasonably protect yourself. Family can defend you in court or at the police station. With money, you can hire a good lawyer to defend yourself. As well, being physically big and muscular can prevent people from even attempting to take advantage of you in the first place. A big stature instils fear into others of physical harm from you.

When society makes it hard to provide for, and protect our families, we cannot blame women for being "gold diggers." Many career-driven women now make more money than their male counterparts. As well, the police can generally protect women, though perhaps not in immediate danger type scenarios. Women are becoming less dependent on men as partners, and the rising cost of living has made it harder to find men who can rise above these societal factors and make enough money to live comfortably. Many millennials are stuck renting basement apartments or living with their mothers even in their thirties or forties.

Women too are not as they once were, as now most women sleep with multiple guys before marriage, and are more focused on their careers rather than being housewives and mothers. Many people will not realize the negative effects which these changes will have on a society and the upbringing of children, until the signs become obvious and it is too late. Morals in future generations will drop, while depression and crime will increase. People will not care about each other in society unless it affects them directly.

When people are struggling to pay their bills, they are not in a peaceful state of mind. They may become desperate and cheat others. When dealing with people, assume that they may be lying about things which are not put in writing. Assume people also do not know what they are talking about, even when they seem very confident or have a very friendly smile, and especially when they are attempting to sell you a product. At the end of the day, it is every man or woman for themselves, and they do not care about you. Often, they care about making a sale, or benefitting somehow by seeming to want to help you. Before hastily signing an agreement, step back, thank them for their time, and do your own research to avoid disappointment and regret. Do this before committing to an investment, vehicle purchase, marriage or other important matter. Do not let them make you feel as though it is a limited time sale, and you must rush to secure it or you might miss out. Often this is a desperate and deceiving sales tactic.

We live in a reactive society where people often take measures to act when it is too little too late. Boastful people will argue with you even when they are wrong. When the signs become clear that they were incorrect, they then may stay quiet, deny it, or say "No one saw that coming." Whoever has the most muscle, influence, money or other form of power, can trample over the rights of others and be defined as being correct. We must realize and accept this to understand how many modern societies work, so that we can avoid having these people cause us undue stress in our lives.

Sometimes, you may even be proven right in an argument with a person or group of people. In which case, do not be harsh with them because they were wrong. Instead, be humble and kind to them after they acknowledge you being correct. If you are too strict with people, they will hate you even though you are correct. Typically, if the person does not owe you anything, it is best to just not argue when they refuse to admit fault. Instead, show your strength by walking away. Focus on your own life and doing what you know is best for you, regardless of what the majority of society says is correct. Often, those in power are able to say and do whatever immoral things they wish, and arguing with them may only cause you more stress.

Policies which protect criminals and punish their victims, are some factors which ultimately can lead to a person taking their own life, after suffering from mental or physical health issues which go unaddressed over a prolonged period of time.[50] If you are facing such issues in the environment which you live in, you can take strategic steps to free yourself from the pain and suffering before you reach your breaking point. For some, the traditional path of consulting with a psychologist may offer some assistance. For others, you can target the root of the problem by making changes to your current lifestyle. This may involve changing careers or relocating far away from the people who brought forth trauma in your life. It can be inconvenient to take the coward approach of running away from your problems. But if the laws in your country are set to defend criminals, and you do not have support from your family or people in influential positions, then you may be better to save what remains of your mental health and move to a better place.[51] A smaller city or town can offer a slower pace of life, where you can recover and heal both mentally and physically. Living in close proximity to nature such as a farmland or ocean can also be beneficial for healing.

Some Western countries which are considered as first world developed nations, have high rates of cancer, mental health issues, mass shootings, homelessness and drug abuse.[52] America for example, is now facing an all-time high rate of suicide among its population.[53] The environmental factors faced by people living in these first world countries, are contributing to first world poverty, where people can drive a decent car and live in a modest house, but struggle to make the monthly loan payments and suffer from health related issues. People may look happy on social media to outsiders, yet they are falling apart and depressed on the inside. Neither wealth nor fame can protect a person from being unsatisfied with their state of being, as even celebrities have committed suicide and overdosed on drugs. We have seen many great civilizations collapse such as the Roman Empire, due to various factors such as the poor long-term planning of unjust rulers, after placing hardship on members of the society.[54]

People of a government and a society must be in general agreement with the primary and secondary goals and values set forth, in order to be efficient and successful. Whether it be health measures such as mask mandates, or temporarily cutting public services to reduce a deficit. In order to strive to be the best, we must work together in harmony, and agree on matters for the better good of the citizens living in a country. We cannot place a burden on a certain segment of the population such as the working middle class, while those with higher income reap much of the rewards. This will leave people disgruntled, and there will be protests and vandalism in the streets.[55] The people who are suffering will not respect the country's agenda, as it does not benefit them in any long-term positive way, and does not align with their own values.

We can work towards having safer and more harmonious communities, by first allowing parents the time and freedom to educate their children with good values at home. These children can then influence their friends through shared positive values amongst themselves. Moreover, neighbours, public service announcements, classroom values instilled in children, and public interactions of community members on a daily basis should all reiterate the same positive and respectful principles. Values such as being honest, not stealing, being respectful and not being aggressive or violent towards innocent members of society. It starts at home from a young age well before the child attends school. No one will care about your child more than you do. Therefore, it is better if one parent can stay home after having a child, in order to raise them right. Afterall, most parents will want better for their children than they do for themselves. This includes having parents teaching their children things which the parents learned throughout their lives.

In order for parents to have the time to spend on the good upbringing of a productive member of society, the parents must first feel financially capable to have one partner stay at home and forego a second household income. In many developed nations, this simply is not a realistic goal for many people. Consequently, the children are raised by babysitters, social media and classmates, while the parents drive three hours a day to and from work. As well, the parents may also need to work a second job or do many hours of overtime, just to make enough money to cover the basic necessities of life.

Multiple surveys in recent years, rank Canada near the very top for satisfaction as one of the best places to live in the world.[56] If you survey many baby boomers and their children who were able to buy houses when the real estate market was more affordable, they might tell you that Canada is a great country to live in. Many of these people are the result of immigration, and will carry great success stories reiterated to their relatives overseas. They may boast of how they were able to successfully establish themselves with hard work in Canada. This then gives more appeal of Canada to immigrants, as it validates opinions which they have previously formed based on movies. Many immigrants imagine a high lifestyle for average people living in Canada, owning big houses and drinking lattes. However, out of the forty million people living in the country, the diversity is huge.[57] If you were to survey younger millennials and youth in the Generation Z age range without a home, you will find the results drastically different.[58]

Many young professionals find themselves moving to other parts of Canada or to the US, due to the rising housing crisis, primarily affecting Toronto and Vancouver.[59] When I raised this concern of increasing housing prices over a decade ago, I was ridiculed as opposing members of society argued with me. They stated that foreign buyers purchasing multiple properties in Canada was good, and they advised me that it was helping the economy. This was years before the term "housing crisis" was common place in the media. This was also years prior to where we are today, where average people are using food banks,[60] university students are sleeping in homeless shelters, and large families are renting cold and dirty basements in Toronto.[61] Unfortunately, that is the best that they can afford while sacrificing their health.

Countries and governments must ensure that their citizens are healthy, safe and protected, so that they may thrive and live comfortably. Using taxpayer dollars, reasonable measures must be implemented, to ensure a nation's residents have basic human rights, such as clean water, stable electricity and basic health care. In addition, residents need to be able to comfortably afford food, clothing, transportation, education and shelter.

Most people want to be happy in life, and the economics related to their present living situation are a big factor of measurement for happiness, stress levels and overall mental wellbeing. A person living in a poorer nation, with dirty drinking water and intermittent electricity, may see their friends and family relocate to Canada and build a mini empire. They then become thrilled at the idea of moving to Canada.[62] They could never imagine that many Canadians must choose between food or rent each month.[63] Little may they know that many Canadian families are now forced to live in the basement of someone else's house, paying rent that covers their landlord's mortgage. Many immigrants have aspired to migrate to Canada, as it is said to be the envy of the world.[64] Upon migrating, many are baffled to see the state in which some are living.

The housing crisis has affected university graduate professionals as well as dual-income young couples alike. By looking at the state of housing and the best-selling car in a certain country, you can grasp a sense of how well the economy is doing. House parties changed to condo parties, and the best-selling car in Canada has been an economy car for the past two decades.[65] Many youths who still strive to own a home in a big city such as Toronto, often now find themselves settling for a small "luxury" condo, instead of the big, detached home their parents once afforded with ease. It is indeed very unfortunate that over half of Canadians who do not currently own a home, have now given up on ever owning one.[66]

Canada is a country rich in resources and consisting of a strong workforce. My solution to assist in improving the economy, would be to develop a national car company. Built by Canadians, for Canadians and the world. The brand would need to be superior in certain areas which would appeal to North Americans as well as other sales regions in the world. For example, it can be very fuel efficient, inexpensive to maintain and backed by excellent customer service. This would help to further industrialize Canada, as well as put Canada on the map for something worthwhile. A Canadian car brand could showcase a technologically advanced, mechanical marvel, which people can admire in car shows worldwide. It could potentially create tens of thousands of jobs and give Canadians something to be proud of.

For many years in Canada, there have been unaddressed issues which Canadians are not proud of. Many Native Indigenous people did not have access to clean water.[67] Young women were reported to have been being sexually assaulted, killed or missing, to which their complaints often went unaddressed.[68] Meanwhile, the ones in charge lived freely on what was once the land of Native Indigenous people. It is a disgrace when a person or group of people, use violence to overpower and control the wellbeing of another person or persons, who cannot defend themselves against the injustice being done to them. The British for example created a diaspora in many parts of the world, where whole new cultures were later formed after people of colonized lands became free.[69] Many Indians and Africans, due to lack of financial means, remained in the countries they were confined to after being taken from India and Africa. People went from being Indian to being West Indian, African to Jamaican, and many other cultures arose from slavery and indentured labour.[70] From pirates, to colonizers, to modern day work slavery, we are controlled by those in power. Often if someone has the power to take advantage of an innocent person without repercussions, they will gladly and selfishly take that opportunity. Therefore, we must safeguard ourselves in order to live healthier, safer, peaceful and more prosperous lives.

Some victims are often afraid to stand up for themselves and be assertive towards their bully or oppressor. They are afraid of being yelled at, afraid of physical violence or afraid of being killed. This is especially true when they do not have a good social network of people supporting them, who they can ask help from should things escalate. So, they feel trapped as though they have nowhere to turn, lacking trust in the legal system if they were to report a big issue, and simply feel as though they have to put up with the other party taking advantage of them. This can apply to kids being bullied at home or in school, a person being raped, abusive relationships, or having a colleague or relative exerting verbal or physical abuse on a person.

The problem is, you may know what happened as well as your oppressor. However, without any witnesses, often times they can lie and even have people support them, whereas you may have no one on your side nor any hard evidence. In these situations, it is often best to try and remove yourself from the toxic environment and save yourself. Try to save up some money and move out, apply to a different school or workplace, or even move out of country if you have no other choice. Another option would be to pull up your pants and fight for your rights defending yourself. If the police do not listen, then take it to the media. Call a decent lawyer who is willing to fight for your case at a reasonable rate. All this can be time consuming, expensive and stressful. Therefore, you must weigh the amount of effort you are willing to put into defending yourself, should you choose to do so. Determine if the possible outcome would be worthwhile in the end.

You may also try to approach your bully and confront them. However, exercise caution when doing so, as this may result in them becoming even more violent with you. Go to the gym, build those muscles and do not let people take advantage of you. Ultimately, it is best to learn from past mistakes, and also try to read people and listen to your intuition on whether a person is up to no good. It is a lot easier to avoid a problem, rather than trying to remedy it afterwards. As the saying goes, an ounce of prevention is better than a pound of cure.[71]

At times we are told the lie that justice and equal rights exist in society.[72] At the end of the day, most human beings are full with lusts, desires, wants, needs and morals or lack thereof. These character traits govern their behaviour in everyday interactions with people. Everyone has their limit of risks they are willing to take in order to try and attain what they want in life. Some act out of selfishness without much care for others. Some act out of desperation in need of life-or-death survival.

I know of a mechanic who makes money doing insurance scams and other illegal activities through his mechanic shop in Toronto. This is a risk he takes, but he is willing to do so to enjoy his luxurious lifestyle with a big house, luxury vehicles, and his kids being privileged to attend private school while his wife stays at home. He weighed the risks in his mind, and felt it is something he is willing to do, knowing what the penalties[73] are if he were to get caught by authorities. I do not recommend this behaviour to anyone, but it is an example of how some are controlled by greed, driving them to take risks to enjoy a certain lifestyle which they desire.

The reason I am advising you of these impulse thought processes certain people have, is to make you aware of how people think, so that you do not let them take advantage of you and cause much unnecessary stress in your life. This same mechanic is my relative, who used violence and threats to steal a large sum of money from me. He then fraudulently used some of the money he stole to buy a car which he signed for. If you cut these dishonest and selfish people out from your life immediately, you might save yourself a lot of time, stress and money later.

After confronting him of the money that he had stolen, he threatened to physically harm me, and warned me not to go to the police at a time when he knew where I lived and had the upper hand over me. He has connections in law enforcement, as well as in the system, with people willing to lie for him. Thus, it would be difficult and potentially very dangerous to pursue such a matter, having the risk of him physically harming me. Unfortunately, for the safety of yourself and your family in such cases, you may need to accept, learn, and move on with your life as best you can without remedy. When you learn the types of motives, values and characteristics a person has, you are able to better predict how far they will push the boundaries of morality and legality to get what they want from you. Avoid places and people involved in criminal activity, even when it is with your own family. They may make you their next victim.

Another example of human nature which may create a problem by imposing on the rights of others, is the natural biological desire of men once they hit puberty. Most women would not understand this, but hormones create strong desires among men, which cause the majority of them to behave differently as compared to if they were not under the influence of their hormonal desires.[74] These impulses can be controlled. However, it has been shown through countless examples in human history, where men unjustly act on these impulsive thoughts, and innocent women fall victim to the overpowering physical strength which the man typically possesses over the woman.

Many countries have strict laws against sexual assault and rape. However, that does not deter some men from still committing acts of terror upon innocent women who happen to be at the wrong place at the wrong time. Often, this leads to a lifetime of torment for the woman as she constantly relives the episode in her head. This may cause another form of injustice to future men she meets. She may hold this incident against them, even though many of these men have no ill intention with her at all.

By understanding the biological thoughts which a typical man naturally has, we can begin to understand his motives and intentions behind actions he may or may not commit in future. This is why I advise women not to walk alone in dark places at night dressed in revealing clothing. It is not the woman's fault, and she should be allowed to dress and go however and wherever she wants, once she is not harming anyone else. However, you need to understand that we do not live in an ideal perfect world. Life is not fair, and opportunists will try and take advantage of us when they have the chance.

Whether it is money, sex, time or energy, we need to safeguard ourselves to prevent people from stripping away from us what we ought to protect. This will save us a great amount of stress, simply by taking precautionary measures in the first place. Therefore, if you are a lady and going to a bar, keep an eye on your drink at all times, do not get too wasted, and have a good friend so you can look out for each other. Yes, in an ideal world you should not need to take these precautions and men should not take advantage of women. But you need to comprehend that this life is not perfect, laws are created by people and are not perfect, and you will not always have someone on your side to defend you. Therefore, we must look out for ourselves and take precautions.

In many first world countries today, we must understand others and what struggles they are facing in life, which may cause them to behave the way they do. If a family is homeless, you may be able to understand why someone is inclined to steal food to feed their family. I am not justifying the behaviour of all criminals, but in certain cases we need to be considerate. However, if a car salesman is already living above the poverty line and his greed causes him to lie to his customers to make a sale, this would be very unethical and selfish of him, and should not be accepted. Yet, they may make a business out of lying, often causing stress for the buyer who gets tricked into paying a significant amount of money, for something that was misrepresented to them. It is often the ones with the most wealth who cheat the innocent, though not always the case.

Keep in mind, humans can be greedy and selfish creatures, and if you are innocent, you may be naive when dealing business with people. You may think that no one can be so dishonest to do something so bad which you cannot imagine, until they do it to you. So always ensure to get things signed and dated in writing when dealing with money and business, even if it is a close relative. Do not feel that making them sign will offend or insult them. Go ahead and insult them, make them sign written contracts. Protect yourself!

Having an avoidable bad experience may cause an individual to lose trust in humanity, and not be so willing to help others nor go into business with people in future. Be mindful that many people are so focused on being financially successful in life, that they lose touch with humanity and act with a lack of ethics. They do not care who you are or what you did for them in the past. They are focused on themselves and their desires. Once they have your money or assets, they are in control of you and the situation, and you may see their bad side which you never imagined.

Many people cheat others out of greed and lack of morals, while some are struggling with societal factors that previous generations did not face. Inflation of food prices and housing, have drastically increased since the rise out of the 2008 world financial crises.[75] Meanwhile, wages did not keep pace with this increased cost of living.[76] People are often stressed and depressed trying to survive, and this may reflect in their attitudes towards their children, spouses and acquaintances. This can lead to tension and resentment in their marriage and family lives, where children feel the parent did not do enough for them. This later reflects on future generations and leads to multiple societal problems such as drug abuse.

If you observe people on a public train or bus in many developed countries, you will see the stressful and tired looks on their faces. The world is an angry place now. Inflation has significantly impacted the lives of people in several developed nations, and people are constantly on edge and ready to attack each other over differences such as race and gender.[77] Along with the prevalence of smartphones as a distraction, people care more about followers and materialistic objects, rather than nurturing the relationships in their lives. At many events now, the majority of people are posting on social media with their phones, rather than living in the moment to heal. Many people are depressed and turn to watching sports and drinking alcohol to escape their stress.

Previous generations had more time in their lives because they had less distractions. Modern conveniences were marketed to make our lives easier, but instead our lives became more complex. Previous generations had less apps, less people to keep in touch with, less lineups waiting for services, and less traffic on the road. People before us spent less time working because they had only one job. You could complete a phone conversation in five minutes that would take approximately twenty-five minutes to type the exact same thing using a smartphone messaging app. Yet the majority insist on the latter. Many people spend over ten hours each week using messaging applications without realizing it. Messaging is far less personal, and can lead to many misunderstandings, as you cannot express the same tone, emotions and facial expressions as you can with face to face or telephone communication.

When people are strained with time and cannot afford to live comfortably, they become insecure and can begin to develop mental health issues. The cost of living is a serious factor related to mental health that is not often considered or talked about. If you look at people living on farms or in villages, you may notice that they have very few belongings, but they are usually smiling and content. In a way, they are the definition of the word community. They help their neighbours, while their children are happy playing together with an old tire and tree branch.

Humans strive to have developed first world nations. Governments take big national loans to build infrastructure, chop down trees that purify the air, and create companies and drive vehicles which further pollute the environment.[78] People traded horses and fresh air for genetically modified fruits, increased cancer rates, and poor mental health.[79] Even the production and disposal of electric vehicles have serious impacts on the environment which will last for future generations.[80] Companies dump tons of chemicals in the ocean, because the fine if they get caught is insignificant compared to the money they save by polluting the fish we eat.[81]

Humans want quick solutions without long-term considerations. Companies shipped manufacturing jobs overseas taking advantage of cheap labour, in exchange for cheap products to buy with money from the jobs we no longer have. People accumulated credit card debt to keep up with things like groceries and rent. Today, both spouses working in many countries is no longer an option, but a necessity. As people are forced to move away from the big cities where their jobs are and buy houses on the outskirts due to rising house costs, they are in turn faced with longer commute times and sacrifice spending time with their children. It seems as mankind has progressed, we encounter more unforeseen circumstances that affect our daily lives and cause us stress.

We are not happy living in little hut houses and living off the land taking only what we need. People value the modern-day assembly line, changing cars every few years and continually buying the latest smartphone. We extract raw materials from the Earth and disturb the intricate balance of the same planet we depend on for future generations. We no longer are content mending and reusing things until they break, but instead fill our homes with cheaply made plastic disposable electronic appliances and gadgets. Large corporations grab our attention with advertisements, convincing us we need things which contribute to child labour and slavery around the world, such as with blood diamonds.[82] They poison our oceans with mercury and tiny plastic pellets in the name of progress. This is part of the cost we pay for big corporations to make the most profit from consumers. Studies have shown that even the drugs people consume end up in their excrement, which in turn ends up in our water supply further affecting wildlife.[83]

Many products we buy now such as furniture and electronics no longer last for decades, but instead last only a little past the warranty period.[84] Corporate greed and people's desire to compete on a materialistic level, has destroyed our planet and damaged our once sustainable natural lifestyle.[85] We as a species, face more stress and mental illness than ever before.[86] This is in addition to the already high cancer rates and chronic diseases that we face. Although we were able to find a cure for many plagues and viruses and are living longer, we are also faced with unfulfilled, depressed lives due to stress and consumerism.[87] Many young people in their thirties now experience anxiety, heart attacks[88] and infertility, which was not nearly as common in previous generations within that age range.[89] We have progressed as a race at the cost of our peace and health.

Not only do individuals contribute to our stresses in life, but also our needs to fit in and compete with others in this rat race we call life. This planet we call home will ultimately be destroyed by ourselves if we do not make extremely drastic lifestyle changes in the next few years. Unfortunately, most humans do not care enough about others to make significant sacrifices in their daily lifestyle. They are more concerned about enjoying their own short stay on planet Earth, without worrying about global warming and polluted oceans. In the end, future generations will continue to suffer and be punished by previous generations.[90]

Many people are too busy following their own desires to care about the harm they do to others. There have been reports of unsuspecting men being cheated by dating overseas women, who have multiple boyfriends in different countries, all of which provide gifts to her and are unknowing of each other.[91] Many men convince women to have sex with them, promising them a long-term relationship leading to marriage. Fake words of love and seductive techniques, induce women to fall emotionally attached and compromise values they have once held close to them. Some women feel obligated to do things for a man physically, because that man has spent money on them, or the man is using his intimidating nature to get what he wants. All of these scenarios are utterly unacceptable, yet relatable to many globally.

As a woman, you do not owe a man anything, such as having sex with him, because he bought you dinner or spent money on you. However, make your intentions clear with him from the start. Do not maintain a gold digger mentality, using guys to buy you expensive dinners and clothing, when you are not attracted to them nor interested in any sort of relationship with them. Be upfront with your intentions prior to recommending that high-end café. Otherwise, do not be surprised if you one day face repercussions from a guy who does not accept being taken advantage of.

It can be difficult to know the true intentions of a person when we deal with them. We are in a societal crisis where even many leaders in communities cannot be trusted with the guardianship of children. Again, there are many good souls out there volunteering and working tirelessly to help the less fortunate and protect the good faith. However, this is directly related to the opportunists who take advantage and cannot be trusted.[92] When a person is raped, has their child murdered or is cheated out of a large sum of money, they often feel helpless, and feel an emptiness inside as they fall into deep depression. All of these traumatic and stressful instances are brought on from other people. Dealing with people on a personal level may immediately affect another person. However, even if you are a board member of a large group, you must realize that your vote counts, and it may affect the lives of many innocent people. Your vote may even prevent a genocide and save thousands of lives.

We must look at ways to protect ourselves from falling into stressful relationships with people, and recover from the pain if we do fall into their traps and have no means of receiving compensation from them. Often times, opportunistic people will take advantage of people who they look at as weak, inferior or otherwise easy prey for them. Victims of opportunistic people may include the young and naive, people who are at a mental disadvantage such as the socially deprived, or those with a mental illness. As well, women, lightweight men and handicapped people can all be targets of opportunistic people. Of course, these perpetrators will not commit horrendous acts in a police station or public place with many cameras and witnesses. They may be your relative, cornering you in the bathroom at a family house gathering. They may be your employer or co-worker, in the evening shift alone with you in the lunchroom.

We must learn not to trust people too easily, as well as look at past examples to realize how easily people can take advantage of others. We can then practice making it a natural habit, to instinctively avoid getting into places and situations where we may fall victim to people with harmful intentions. If you were raised by controlling parents which resulted in you being a pushover, it may be hard to speak up even as you watch someone do harm to you, such as rape or fleece you. Many passive individuals suffer from a lifetime of devastation because of an act that happened to them decades ago. If you happen to be in a situation where you see a person about to be violated, and you have the means and capacity to prevent the culprit from committing the act of harm, you should do what you can to stop it. Either physically or verbally act, to prevent the offender from taking advantage of their victim. You may lead the victim to be forever grateful to you for preventing them a lifetime of pain and suffering.

People who are docile, too submissive, and people pleasing pushovers, are often afraid of confrontation which may include them getting yelled at or violently attacked. In their minds, it seems easier to comply with the bully, whether it be their parents, partner or business associate. They may helplessly witness themselves being violated, and just feel obligated to give a fake smile or laugh, so that the violator does not become angry if they were to stand up for themselves. Though, many people may not understand this, as the majority of the population may not suffer from this fate and mindset.

Studies have shown in history, that people who are hired in positions of power, are often taller individuals or males.[93] In some cases, you would need to be a certain height in order to qualify to become a police officer, which would lead to disqualifying many women the opportunity of being hired for this role.[94] As well, police officers in most countries are given privileges and rights not given to the general public. Combine a person who has grown up with a bigger physical stature than most, with a badge of authority, and it may be dangerous if they were to abuse their power with their victims who have little or no recourse. We have seen numerous cases where this has proven true, where people of colour or a certain religion, have been targeted victims of violence from the few prejudice police officers.[95] This unfortunately gives the rest of good police officers a bad reputation.[96]

When police or someone in a position of authority abuses their power, it can instill fear and anxiety within their victims. Just seeing a police car pass by can cause a person to have a panic attack, though the person is not doing anything unlawful.[97] This is reflective of past experienced trauma. We need to be cautious of people who crave power, and act without any common sense ethics to preserve a person's dignity or human rights. Some even get away with murder due to the position of power they are in.[98] Violence, biasness, racism and prejudice are still existent in many cultures and societies, so we must learn to protect and defend ourselves, without getting ourselves in trouble.

If you do end up in a situation where someone is committing an act which brings harm to you, intentional or unintentionally, you can begin by trying to confront them in a stern tone. Verbally communicating that their behaviour is unwanted and will not be tolerated. If you fear they may become physically violent with you, speak in a peaceful manner and discuss it with them. Different situations will require different tactics of speaking to a person.

In a marriage, it is best to privately discuss things together about each other. As fun as it may seem, you should never insult or defame your spouse while you are in the company of others, regardless if your spouse is present or not. When you speak ill about your friend or partner, it demonstrates to others that you do not value or respect that person. This can lead to others laughing about you and your significant other behind your back. It can also open the door for conniving, opportunistic people to take advantage of yourself or your spouse, knowing that the two of you are not in a harmonious and respectful relationship. For example, they may secretly ask your spouse for money and advise them not to tell you about it, or they could secretly flirt with your partner behind your back. In marriage, you need to be on the same team with your partner and have honest and open conversations with one another.

Chapter 4: Relationships, Marriage and Divorce

In life, a friend, spouse or other person that is close to you might hurt you unintentionally. In this case, you should immediately raise the concern to them gently, so that they are aware of their actions and how it has affected you. Bringing things out in the open early on, will give you both the opportunity to realize the cause and effect of the situation, and how to work on things to make it better for both of you. This can potentially save much stress over the long-term, and even save the friendship or relationship.

Your partner may be completely oblivious as to how their actions are annoying you. Such as having the temperature on very high in the car or picking their teeth while you two are enjoying a meal. However, if you bring this up to them from the beginning, it allows the person to realize how their actions have impacted you or made you feel. This way, you can both discuss, compromise, and adjust these little behaviours in your lives, for a more fruitful and enjoyable experience together. Do not assume people understand your feelings on any matter. People are not mind readers. Sometimes little things can turn into big issues down the road, so it is better to bring everything out in the open early on, rather than hear about it ten years later when one party threatens divorce.

Some people may try and manipulate a situation to make you feel guilty, as though you are the problem. Assess the situation clearly to determine the causes and effects. In some instances, you both may be at fault! In cases of anger management issues, we must tread lightly. If possible, have the person attend counselling with you and address these issues. In relationships, if one person is constantly yelling and being aggressive, then out of fear, the other person no longer feels entitled to voice their own opinions. Some women in an abusive relationship, or children dealing with family members, may be quiet when someone physically bigger is taking advantage of them. They do not speak up and do not complain out of fear of being cussed down or hit. This is the case with many children from abusive households, as well as people who have controlling and abusive bosses or partners.

Do not stay in an abusive relationship out of fear, nor think that they will change after numerous times. Take precautions, prevent them from knowing your new address in order to avoid retaliation, change your number and block them on social media. Desperate times call for desperate measures, and sometimes the ones we love hurt us the most. This can be in part because they never cared for us the same way we cared for them. Their superior position being the parent, spouse or employer, allowed them to take advantage of us and hurt us. They did not feel any pain, so they do not care how we feel. Remember that.

With certain people, bringing up something such as a bad habit they have, or confronting them about something they lied to you about, may cause them to lash out verbally or physically towards you. In such instances, avoid these people in your life if possible. However, if life dictates that you cannot simply block certain people out of your life, you must carefully and gently communicate a few selected things you would like to bring to their attention. Although you may not deserve it, nor be the cause of their toxic behaviour, it is how they are, so we must learn to deal with these sorts of individuals in life. It is an unfortunate truth, many are oblivious to their own flaws, and refuse to improve their negative character traits such as rude behaviour, lying or becoming physically aggressive towards others. They see this as acceptable behaviour, even though they would not like someone to lie or become aggressive towards them. These people are the ones who become defensive no matter how politely you try to point out their flaws. Tread lightly, and swiftly correct them if you get the opportunity.

Few people in this world actually appreciate constructive criticism, to take it upon themselves to improve their character and bad habits, without the thought of financial or other benefit. Many humans are selfish, and when they see a suffering child in another country, they will happily watch their favourite series instead. Things would need to reach the point where it dominates the media and thousands are massacred, before many people care about the suffering of others. Especially if it is affecting a race or religious group of people whom are portrayed negatively by their oppressors.

It is sad to say, but many rich people in the world, though not all, obtained their wealth from cheating and scamming the middle class and even poor individuals. They will happily take the last $5 that someone has, so that they can add an additional $5 to their massive empire of wealth. Many business owners cheat individuals using false product promises and lies to deceive. Scammers use social engineering and conning techniques while showing confidence, and will even swear oaths to others stating that they are being honest, when in reality they are far from telling the truth. Thus, it makes it increasingly difficult to find someone you can truly trust for a life partner, who will genuinely care about you unconditionally without selfish motives for their personal gain.

As divorce rates in Western countries have increased, most no longer live in farmland communities.[99] Parents and society over a century ago would allow, and often encourage people to get married in their teenaged years.[100] Life was a simpler time, where men and women had more defined roles in society. Men were the hunters, gatherers and sole providers for the home. Women would take care of the home and the family by cooking fresh meals and looking after the young children. Older children would do chores and help on the farm with the animals and land. The internet and dating apps based on superficial traits did not exist. People were forced to interact with strangers, such as asking for directions to the nearest petrol station. People met in more conventional ways, such as at school, places of worship, the market or a coffee shop. parents would also suggest matches for their children based on who was respectable in the community. Cheating and divorce were shunned by society and far less common than it is today.

Before cellphones became the norm, you would be forced to give out your parents' home phone number. For the sake of not wanting to seem like a hoe or a player, you would not give your number to more than one or two people of the opposite gender at a time. Then, when your love interest would call home, your parents would give them a brief interview prior to advising you to pick-up the phone.

"Do you smoke?"

"What education and job do you have?"

After which, they might ask you about this person, and eventually want to meet them if you wished to continue going out with them. Having parents involved from such an early stage in the relationship, forced people to take the relationship more seriously. The term "ghosting" did not exist, and people worked harder to make relationships work.[101]

In the early 1900's, couples would get married and buy a house, or obtain some farmland from their parents to start their way in life. People themselves were much simpler as the world was more isolated. Most people living in the same town often listened to the same music, not knowing what was available on the other side of the globe. When the television came into existence, most watched the same few programs available to them at the time. People were healthier, more relaxed, and easier to talk to.[102]

In many small towns, reputation was important, as everyone knew one another and few travelled out of town often. Things like celibacy were much more common and respected in society, as it was a form of dignity and decency.[103] Families would regularly attend church or their religious place of worship together. These are values people held dear to them which upheld the moral fabric of society. Therefore, when a couple got married, they had far less baggage, and marriage was more than just a signature on a piece of paper, as it often seems is the case today. Just a few decades ago, partners would take the time to get to know each other for their character and morals. They would devote their time only knowing that one person, and naturally fall in love, accepting their flaws and not caring about anyone else romantically.

In today's society, life is much more complex and fast-paced. As society has progressed, so has the complexity of our relationships and problems that come along with them. We feel time crunched, and lack the energy and patience required to invest in a healthy and romantic relationship. It often seems easier to throw away our spouse and get a new one as a quick fix, the way we throw out our old socks instead of mending them. We think that we can find someone better who does not have the same bad traits that our existing partner has, and we focus on any minor imperfections in our current relationship. However, we are often deceiving ourselves, and end up with someone who has many other worse characteristics, such as poor money management, lying, and sleeping around while they say they were working late. We must realize that no one is perfect, so we must communicate and compromise in life to make relationships work.

Today, dating apps have created a fictional mindset of the ideal partner for people who are not top-tier themselves. Morbidly obese women are looking for six-foot-tall male doctors, with good manners and the body of a professional athlete. Over eighty percent of women are targeting the top twenty percent of men, and there is only so much to go around.[104] Social media has influenced women to believe that they can have a rich guy who still has plenty of time to spend with them. Though, in most cases this is not realistic. If you are a woman who desires abundant attention from your partner, and you want him home by 6 p.m. to have dinner with you, then you should not expect your husband to provide you with a very luxurious lifestyle. The reason is that for a man to achieve financial success, he will likely need to devote countless hours working or growing his business to obtain his wealth. This would mean of course, less time spent with you. Some women are okay with this, some are not. Therefore, you must be realistic and know that you cannot have it all in most cases.

To change this ideology for the betterment of society, we must realize that social media and dating apps are often not reality. Do not idolize celebrities nor believe in influencers who seem very wealthy and happy. Many will rent supercars and film themselves on jets which they do not own, in order to promote themselves or their products.[105] To live such an extravagant lifestyle in reality, often a person must be selfish and take advantage of others. Therefore, if they were doing so well for themselves, why would they wish to share their secrets or help others. Be cautious, as it might be a way for them to profit off you by selling their classes in a get-rich-quick scheme. Do not get caught up in over-hyped status symbols. You could end up losing money instead of saving. Do not believe in what you see on social media. Advanced photo filters can make women look slim with flawless skin, and make men look equally more attractive. With artificial intelligence, you may fall in love with someone who is completely non-existent, with a fully synthesised character and artificial voice.[106]

We must realize that we live in a very promiscuous time, where many women are sleeping around with the same few men in many metropolises. There have been online pages dedicated to determine if two women are dating the same guy, which proves that this is a problem.[107] Hookup culture and dating apps have massively contributed to this epidemic of widespread, temporary fulfilment of sexual desires, with no commitment.[108] Swipe on Thursday, sleep together on Friday, and never call each other again. This has become the norm in many big Western cities worldwide. Meanwhile STDs (sexually transmitted diseases) have run rampant.[109]

People now want the ideal person, as they see endless potential matches on dating apps and think that they can always do better. A woman will match with one tall athletic guy, one rich guy, one smart guy and one funny guy. She then will get false hopes and desires that she can find her ideal man with all of these qualities combined, when he simply does not exist. If a man is of the most desirable one-percent, he is not interested in the majority of women for a serious commitment, which may include yourself. Self-realization can be a harsh reality to face, but a necessary reality in order to move forward and progress in life. If you do not wish to be forty years old, going into menopause, and living alone in your apartment with several cats; then consider avoiding dating apps all together, and look for your spouse outside of major metropolitan areas. More rural areas will often yield better results if you are looking for someone more traditional with less baggage. An increasing number of men are also turning outside of their cities, and going overseas to look for wives as they join the passport bros movement.[110] If you are financially stable, and have traditional values, you may wish to consider this option as well.

Often, the men and women from foreign countries may come with their own challenges. These may include language barriers, low standards for education and differences in cultural norms. Certain cultures will typically produce women with more feminine qualities, who have skills such as cooking taught to them by their mothers. They may be taught to respect their husbands, and not mix with the opposite gender outside of family relations. These societies have more traditional roles where the man is expected to fully support the household financially, and the woman can stay at home to raise children. Very different than Western society, where it has become mandatory to have two incomes simply to survive in many large cities.

We have reached an epidemic due to the rising housing costs, where couples are waiting longer to get married or not getting married at all.[111] People wish to finish university, get a job in their field, save for their wedding then save for a house. By this time, they are well into their thirties. If they manage to get married, they may face age and environment related issues, needing IVF (In Vitro Fertilization) to assist in having a baby. After which, they have less energy and time to spend raising their child. Families have shrunk from having three or more kids, to now barely having more than one.[112] You have to decide what you want in life, what you are willing to contribute and sacrifice, and where the best options for you to live would be.

One of the best times and places to meet your life partner is when you are in school. It may be a high school sweetheart or university classmate, which can result in a very loving life-long marriage. The longer you wait, the harder it is to meet someone who is without an STD or a child. You do not need a house or a university degree to get married, as you can work on accomplishing these things and building your life together during the marriage. Be especially grateful if you have understanding parents, who are kind enough to let you live under their roof, until you finish university and obtain a stable job. Though sadly, many parents do not understand how difficult it is to meet driven people with good values today. So, they will simply tell you that you are too young to get married, and let you fall into the societal trap to realize there are not many good options when you hit thirty-years-old.

A person practicing celibacy was once considered the norm, then in later generations it was the respected minority in society, and now those waiting for marriage would often be embarrassed to openly admit so. They may be questioned as to why they are waiting, such as if it were for their religious beliefs or other reasons. Sex before marriage was once concealed, but is now something promoted in society which people boast about. The long-term effects this has on the fabric of society is endless and can cause a strain on families. In order to live a peaceful life, we need to shift the thinking of society to a point where people respect each other and respect themselves.

We need laws to enable citizens to legally protect themselves. In some places, it can even be possible to sue another person for sleeping with your spouse.[113] Criminalizing cheating for married couples would lead to a lower divorce rate, as people would know the financial and legal consequences if they were to be unfaithful. Many people cheat because they think their partner will not find out. However, think about the moral aspect of it and ask yourself, would you want your daughter to marry a dishonest cheating guy such as yourself? If this is you, perhaps you should reconsider your lifestyle and the impact it has on multiple families. Your fling's partner may never look at them nor love them the same once they find out they had another man inside of them. Their children may lose all respect for them and begin to abuse them after an affair. This goes for men and women. Cheating can set a bad influence in families and society, and many think it is harmless fun until it happens to them. If you are not happy in the relationship and there is no way of adding excitement to rekindle the love, do not cheat. Instead, you may consider leaving your partner, especially if they are abusive. It might not always be easy, especially if you have children. Research the best options available, such as government assistance programs to support single parents, or even move in with your parents after divorce if you have that option.[114]

We are an advanced race with technology connecting us more than ever. Yet, this has caused us to be far less connected with each other, and we lack the bonds formed together which once brought us peace. Deactivating your social media account, or unfollowing random people from the opposite gender, may be the best move you make to fix your relationship or maintain a healthy marriage. Many marriages today end in divorce due to social media and false impressions of what marriage should be like.[115] Many influencers post their fairy tale lives, living as the one percent. They often fail to show the arguments and ugliness behind the scenes. Even billionaires and princes cannot seem to keep up with their wives' expectations of marriage in modern society. As well, the wedding itself has become a competition between relatives and friends, trying to outdo each other with the most flamboyant wedding. Though statistics show, lower cost weddings often lead to a lower divorce rate.[116] Yet, couples still feel the urge to dive into deep debt in order to show off to their guests for their one-day of fame. Imagine the embarrassment when the marriage fails as it often does, within the first six months, and having to split the wedding debt among you and your ex-spouse. It will be a grim reminder of the one-day event you may regret, as you take years to pay off the debt. A simple wedding is a blessed one, and you can use the excess money saved towards your future in marriage, such as taking trips together and building memories. Building debt ultimately leads to a strain in the marriage, and delays the time needed to save for a home, retirement or your child's education.

Once you are married, be respectful to your partner and the role they play in your life. When you continue to go out with close "friends" of the opposite gender, you are taking away time and energy that you should be investing in your actual life partner. The laughter, hugs and jokes you share with someone else, may make you become confused when you are with your actual partner. You may slip up, thinking you told your partner a joke or what happened at work that day, then realize it was something you shared with your close guy friend. You may consider these guy friends as brothers, who will protect you when you are hanging out. Though typically, those same guy friends are just waiting for their chance to get into your pants. The girl is often shocked when one of those guys who she thinks of as a brother, asks her out and confesses his romantic interest in her.

There are exceptions, where a guy and girl genuinely share very similar moral values, and have matching personalities where they are very good friends with no ulterior motives. However, generally with most guys, they want to date, marry or have sex with you. This is why it is very dangerous to complain to random people about your little problems that you have in your marriage. I say marriage, but this can apply to common-law or other partner relations as modern society dictates. Male friends are often happy to hear you cry about your husband's snoring or other bad habits, so that they can console you, hug you, and use soft words of encouragement to seduce you.

"You deserve better than him."

"You are such a pretty girl. You can have any guy you choose if you left him."

Meanwhile, we all have flaws, social media is often fake, and people will happily put on an act of their best behaviour during the dating phase. The key to a successful marriage is to work on things calmly together with your spouse, without reaching out to outsiders for help, unless the relationship is abusive or you and your spouse cannot compromise and agree on things.

Discuss little annoyances openly with your spouse when they arise, before they grow into bigger problems. Tell them you do not like it when they leave their dirty dishes in the sink, or when they leave their smelly gym socks all over the place. Compromise to make each other happy, as this can in turn make yourself happy and have the other person's love for you grow. As the saying goes, "Happy wife, happy life."

Treat your wife to date nights once a week, or however often you can afford to in order to keep things interesting in the marriage. After being married for years, things can get boring both in the bedroom and in daily routines. Take trips together and leave the kids with the grandparents for a week if you can. Vacations often bring out an adventurous side of people which relieves stress and builds memories together. Your spouse should be your best friend whom you trust more than anyone else in life. Aim to be inseparable through these connective bonds and experiences, so you do not ever think of looking for love elsewhere.

As much as women may not like to admit it, they generally gossip a lot. However, one thing you should never mention to others, is about what goes on in the bedroom. If you wish to have a peaceful and successful marriage, your sex life should remain private with your partner. You can try new things and discuss areas to improve on together with your spouse. However, it is also important to overcome past traumatic experiences in your life, as depression can affect your sexual performance. This can ultimately leave your partner unfulfilled, which can cause both of you to be in a constant cranky mood. Unfortunately, some parents then proceed in taking this frustration out on their children, such as constantly yelling at them unjustly. Finally, if there is an addiction or other sexual health related concern in the marriage, consult with a professional, such as a medical doctor or counselor.

Men like and crave sex. It is a deeply built-in, biological desire. Men may even think irrationally when they are horny, comparable to being drunk.[117] Therefore, having regular sex with your husband, will often keep him happy and satisfied with you so he will not seek it elsewhere. Although of course, there are the bad boys who will always cheat, even if you do not withhold sex in the marriage. In some instances, this escalates with the more money a man makes, as he feels entitled to have more women because he feels as though he deserves it.[118]

To prevent this, I highly recommend signing a marriage contract prior to marriage, stating that if your partner cheats, you can divorce and have them pay you a penalty. If possible, and as per your preference, you should include things such as, your spouse cannot marry a second spouse while you two are married. As well, disallowing your spouse from working in certain jobs such as online sex chat services. Furthermore, you can include financial terms, such as being able to keep all of your existing assets and wealth, which you acquired prior to the marriage, should a divorce materialize.

Just as in life, it is important to handle constructive criticism maturely, and realize when your partner is gently telling you about your negative traits. They tell you the truth because they care about you, and they want to love you harder and for longer. Instead of becoming defensive and making up excuses for your shortcomings, look into ways you can work on your deficiencies. Jump on that treadmill and work on your diet. Control your anger and tell your partner that you love and appreciate them. Learn their love language, and do things in support of what they will appreciate.[119] Show interest and support their passions, provided it is not harmful to any innocent being. If you have a fight during the day, remember that every marriage has its own challenges and disagreements. Apologize, and have some healthy makeup sex.

Discuss issues calmly while falling asleep together in bed and try to understand things from your partner's viewpoint. Do not merely pretend to listen to them, while you are in reality just waiting for them to finish talking so that you can say what is on your mind. Forgive the little mistakes they may have done, and if you made the mistake, promise to never intentionally make the same mistake again and take steps towards achieving this. It is often much cheaper and less stressful to work on your existing marriage, rather than find someone new to repeat the process. If you cannot work things out privately together after trying repeatedly, then seek an unbiased mediator, who can provide insight and advice for the best approach to move forward. Divorce should be the absolute last resort in the marriage, and not seen as an easy way out.

Prior to marriage, it is important to assess compatibility, instead of simply marrying someone who you find physically attractive and funny. Marriage is more than a friendship; it is a partnership. Like going into business with someone, it is imperative that you assess compatibility to ensure you share similarities on important matters. These should include, religious beliefs, money management and finances, hygiene, children upbringing if you choose to have kids, as well as daily lifestyle and long-term goals. Are you a spender but she is a saver? Do you like to go out often, and he prefers cuddling on the couch with a movie and home cooked meal? These things that may not matter much while dating, can break apart a marriage while living in the same household. Hence why you should ask important questions concerning your life together before it is too late. Things such as religious views with raising your children, family values, how you will spend the holidays, and the frequency of vacations should be discussed. It may seem like an interview process, but it is a lot less stressful and cheaper than divorce.

When looking for a partner, seek someone you find peace in, not someone who takes away your peace. A virtuous woman is the best blessing a man can have in life. A supportive great woman can help a man be stronger and more successful. Conversely, a bad woman can ruin a man's life, and make him homeless or want to commit suicide. You must choose wisely when selecting a life partner now more than ever.

A good marriage will make you yearn for your spouse while you are at work. If you find yourself working later and longer hours, meeting with friends, or going out by yourself to avoid spending time at home with your spouse; this may mean that your spouse is taking away your peace, and you are avoiding them to maintain your sanity in life. In this scenario, try to pinpoint what you do not like about the marriage and your spouse. Write it down and consider why things may be the way they are.

Many people tell you that it does not matter who started the conflict first. This is to force you to accept the oppressive behaviour and force you to shut up about it. In reality, it is extremely important to determine who and what caused the conflict in order to come to a peaceful and fair resolution. Is your spouse upset at you because you slept with your boss at last year's holiday party? So now they constantly nag you about little things such as not squeezing the tube of toothpaste to their preference? Did you sincerely apologize, and try your best to make things right between you and your partner? Or perhaps they come from a spoiled upbringing, and expect things too highly of you, such as designer bags and luxury vehicles. All while not offering much in the marriage themselves. Whatever the reason, discuss things with your spouse calmly, so that you can both acknowledged the areas of concern and address them.

In a healthy marriage you work together as one body, one team and one powerful force. Never put each other down nor slander each other's name in public, family gatherings or elsewhere; regardless if your partner is around or not. Never deliberately insult each other, and do not do sneaky things behind your partner's back which you would not want done to you. Jump up and wrap your legs around your husband to greet him when he returns home, even if you had a big fight the night before. Keep yourself clean, while looking and smelling good for your spouse. This is far more important than looking good for your co-workers and friends. Keep your facial hair in a fashion which pleases your partner. These little things go a long way in the relationship, and when you quarrel, they may forgive you sooner and more easily because they find you more attractive.

Consult with each other prior to making big purchases or doing home renovations, even if you are using your own money and not your partners. When you communicate and trust each other, you become an unstoppable team. With this, you can prosper and accomplish great things in marriage and in your life. Good vibes will begin to flow throughout your life. On the other hand, when you have a spouse who you do not trust, and you are constantly worried over their actions; you will lack the confidence and motivation needed to do much in life, and you will not make the effort to succeed as you should.

Conceal your partner's flaws. Make excuses to cover for each other, such as if your spouse does not want to attend your aunt's third wedding during a big sports game. Be open and honest with each other so you can build unbreakable trust together. However, be sensitive when your wife asks you if her food tastes good or if she looks fat in her dress. You may avoid the truth in this particular scenario and compliment her in order to preserve the marriage. Women can be sensitive while needing to feel secure, and men must understand this. Men and women are biologically created different, and think differently in a way which can complement each other. In the case of an emergency, such as during a pandemic where you will be forced to quarantine together twenty-four hours a day for months; it will be far more enjoyable doing it with someone you love and trust, rather than someone you despise. If you try to lie and hide things, the other person can only turn a blind eye for so long before they eventually consider leaving you.

Divorce rates in many big cities are now over fifty percent.[120] Many divorces are caused by infidelity, finances, and in-laws. With in-laws, it is often the mother-in law in some cultures who contributes most to the divorce.[121] Often times, mama's boys will side with their mother if there is ever a disagreement between his mother and his wife. This biased and unfair practice can happen regardless if his mother is right or wrong. Keep in mind, when a girl marries a man, she is leaving the protection and provision of her father, so her husband then takes on this responsibility. My recommendation is to not live with your in-laws after marriage if possible, and not have in-laws meddle in your marriage. If your wife and mother have a disagreement, it is important to look at the situation fairly, without bias, and decide who is the most logical person in that instance. Then kindly explain to the other party, either your wife or mother, why you believe they are wrong. Sometimes two people have different preferences of doing things which accomplish the same result, and neither way of doing the task is incorrect. Also be careful who you discuss your marriage issues with. Some relatives and so-called friends have cruel and jealous intentions. Other elders may wish to help but instead make things worse with old village mentality, inapplicable to modern marital affairs.

Being in a long-term relationship can be one of the most beautiful, yet challenging adventures you embark on in life. Differences in cultures and upbringing can add value, diversity and beauty to a marriage. These differences in cultures can also take patience and understanding to appreciate and adapt to. Marriage is a difficult journey on its own, so do not further complicate things by listening to the horrible advice of outsiders. Such as girlfriends telling you that your husband should spend more time and money on you, when he is already doing his best, providing you with a reasonably comfortable lifestyle as it is.

Often women will marry a man for his wealth and status. However, this can be very dangerous as this is not love. Wealth can vanish, looks can fade, and good public figure standing can be tarnished by one false allegation or legitimate affair that goes public. Women must realize, in their beauty and purity, holds much of their value, as shallow as that is in our society. They can use it to sell their bodies online and become millionaires who no one wants to marry. Or they can use it to catch the most decent, upright, intelligent man who they invest a future in. Regardless if you marry your spouse for their looks or wealth, you need to have shared values with money, ethics, health, lifestyle and future plans, so that you do not get into big disagreements. You need to plan ahead together and live within your means to avoid downfall in the next recession.

Understand that your relationship with your partner is more important than your job that pays you. Do not be helpful and pleasant with those outside of your household more than the kindness which you show to your own spouse and children. Invest more time with your own family if you want to be successful. Some men will work multiple jobs plus overtime, barely being home with their wife. The man will think that he is doing a good thing, by making more money to spend on his wife for vacations and jewelry. In reality, his wife is lonely and disgruntled, because her man is always tired, and cannot perform his duty in bed. In this case, if you are already making enough money to live comfortably, realize that you only have one life to live, and you cannot take your money with you when you die. Live the best life you can and enjoy your healthy days with your partner. Work on building the important bond and joyful memories together.

If you are struggling with your work-life balance, it may be that you are trying to keep up with living a lifestyle which is beyond your means. For example, if you have a big mortgage and high car payments, consider downsizing your home to a more affordable one. As well, stop financing luxury vehicles that you cannot afford to buy cash. Settle for a less expensive or second-hand car, until you may afford the car you really desire later on. Many people do not like to be told what they can and cannot buy. However, it is far better to live a simple, less lavish life within your means, rather than cause stress to yourself and everyone around you when money is tight. With the cost of living in major cities around the world increasing, many may find it difficult to survive on just one income.[122] Therefore, it is important to discuss expectations and the responsibility of each spouse prior to getting married. Ask important questions about their lifestyle, values and goals such as follows.

What things upset them and how do they control their anger?
Would they want to share social media and banking passwords or keep them private?
Are they a spender or a saver?
Do they have any debt?
Do they give in charity?

How do they handle stress?

Do they have any passions and hobbies?

Do they want to have children?

Do they prefer a night out or prefer to stay in?

Why did their last relationship end?

Do they have any close friends of the opposite gender?

How do they see a typical day in marriage?

Do they smoke or drink alcohol and does this align with your lifestyle?

Do they suffer from any serious health issues and will you be willing to work with them on this?

Do they exercise and keep a healthy lifestyle?

Do they have any annoying traits such as snoring?

For what reasons would they consider ending the relationship?

What are their values regarding sex before marriage?

What are their reasons to get into a serious relationship with you?

What kind of wedding would they like and do your expectations align with this?

Will your spouse stay home after children, and will your income be enough to support the household?

What role might their parents play in your marriage?

What role will religion play in your lives together, and do you share the same beliefs? How will this influence your future children together?

Where will you move to if you purchase a home together?

What are their retirement goals?

Asking these serious and unromantic questions can help you decide if you wish to proceed with a committed relationship together. Finance and family values are among the most important.

Discuss who will do what chores. Some parents do not ask their children to do house chores, because they want their kids to focus on their homework. When these children grow up and get married, both people depend on the other person to do house chores in the relationship, or they may end up living in filth. Some men expect to never do any chores, but they bring in a high salary. I am not saying this is right or wrong. You must discuss expectations, and come to a mutual understanding with who will provide what in the marriage. When the romance slows down, fundamental and mutual understanding can help you thrive.

This life is short, but too long to be living alone. If you decide marriage is something you want, make sure you are prepared to pull your weight. Do not expect your spouse to do everything for you such as a mother or maid would do. Some parents spoil their children which later creates challenges in marriages for their children's partners. Talk to your children maturely from babies as though they are adults. Take them places and explain things to them about life, such as at the grocery store and educating them on financial literacy. Teach them one plus one equals two, instead of gaa-gaa, goo-goo.

Marriage can be a blissful journey or a living nightmare. The easiest way to prevent marriage stress, is to not marry a person whose character and personality traits mismatch yours. Primarily with things such as financial values, hygiene, daily lifestyle, human rights views, religious beliefs and goals. It is alright if your partner or potential partner does not share the same tastes in music and food as you do. When you love someone, you may even adapt to begin liking the same music and try new foods in appreciation of them. Marry someone you feel comfortable being with, and whom you do not feel the need to put on an act while in front of them. You should feel comfortable being yourself in a relationship and feel at peace. However, if you married only a pretty face or fat wallet instead of going for matching characteristics, then you must look for ways to mesh your different values, goals and lifestyles together, in order to make the marriage work.

When facing conflict or annoying habits in a relationship, specify what differences and negative traits you dislike about each other. Then rank them by level of tolerability in the relationship. Little habits such as chewing with your mouth open and leaving the toilet seat up, can be corrected with positive reinforcement and a little effort. This activity requires two people who are willing to put in the effort to make the relationship work. If one or both of you have anger management issues, then you will not have much progress, and should comprehend that you need to control your anger if you wish to progress in life and not end up in jail.

Address the deal-breakers that you cannot stand about your partner, and verbally communicate with each other on whether you are each willing to correct your negative traits. This is for the behaviours and attributes which a person can adjust. If you married a short guy and now decide you want to have someone over six feet tall, you cannot expect your partner to do an operation to extend his height suddenly. However, if he has a bad habit of chatting to other girls on social media and flirting, or you go out shopping and stay out late without telling him, then these are things you can each work on. If you are unwilling to change, do not expect a positive change in the marriage. Instead, expect stress, secrets, lies and possible cheating. After which, divorce may be inevitable.

Communicating with your spouse is one of the most important things you can do to have a successful marriage, and it must be mutual. Speak to your spouse every single day and let them know what things are bothering you. Share with them interesting ideas you have. Make them aware of the things in life which you are looking forward to, both short-term and long-term. This way, you both can build a lifestyle together with your goals in mind. Tell them jokes or happy things you experienced in your day. Do not only speak to the cute guy or girl at your workplace about things in your life, then go home with a frown while not speaking to your spouse.

If you have had some difficulty that has damaged the relationship to the point where communication is now at a minimal; try to speak with your partner a little bit more each day, until they hopefully begin to open up with you also. Tell them about problems you are facing and things that are bothering you in the relationship. Be kind and gentle when discussing things. Do not yell and cause them to form resentment towards you. If you feel you are beginning to become angry, back away and resume the conversation in the near future, when you both are calm and collected.

Divorce should never be used as a threat to force your partner to give in to your demands. Some cultures and religions even prohibit a married couple from being divorced.[123] It really is until death does you apart. In other cultures, it is allowed, but shunned by the community.[124] In the Islamic faith, divorce is allowed but the least liked of allowed things.[125] In many South Asian communities, the thought of a divorced woman is that of used or damaged goods, whom would be second choice at best. A girl may be single and beautiful in her young twenties, having endless choices of guys for marriage. But the moment she is divorced, she is immediately limited to a small fraction of potential candidates in conservative communities. In such instances, it can be useful for a woman to be independent. As a woman, educate yourself so that you can support your child and yourself, should you go through a divorce. This will prevent you from feeling obligated to stay with an abusive partner for financial support.

There are many men who have great wives, yet somehow find the need to cheat and treat their wives badly. Many men marry women for purity and beauty and want a girl who is a virgin. Yet, when they have this in their hands, they are not content with her, and look at other women to have an affair with. Infidelity can be one of the most daunting tasks to deal with in a marriage. It can lead to spouses no longer trusting each other and ultimately getting divorced, as some find it unforgivable. When you invest time, effort, money and your heart into a relationship, the other person has emotional control over you. You may not realize this if you are in love. This is why you get hurt so much if the person cheats on you. It is perfectly acceptable and natural to fall in love with someone. But think with your brain as well as your heart when selecting a partner for a committed relationship. Ensure that your values align.

Men look for outward beauty, and women look for security and protection. We no longer live in caves fighting off animals in the wild. We now mostly live in cities, where money is the form of security for people. In some regions of the world, women are responsible for initiating approximately seventy percent of divorces.[126] These ratios are intensified in Western cultures, where promiscuity and adultery are prevalent, and divorcing a hardworking guy can be incentivized by governmental policies and the judicial systems. Many Western countries grant each partner fifty percent of total wealth and assets upon divorce.[127] As well, a woman can demand child and spousal support to continue maintaining her high level of lifestyle after the marriage.[128] This can potentially make an undeserving man become homeless, and his driver's license may become suspended once he misses making the payments to his ex-wife, which can prevent him from getting to his job on time to earn an income.

A woman may file for divorce after her husband loses his job if he can no longer provide the luxurious lifestyle which she has become accustomed to. Some women may even forgive cheating. However, do not expect many women to stay if you cannot protect her, nor provide her with the standard of living which she thinks she deserves. Especially if she is beautiful and has multiple options of other men sending her private messages through social media. Many women cannot cook well and are not virgins before marriage. Yet, they consider themselves high-value women, and demand more from men today than ever before in previous generations. This is the unfortunate reality we must deal with in woke times.

In divorce, many Western judicial systems disregard concerns over which partner owned the assets or monetary value before the marriage, as well as concerns over whom accumulated it during the marriage.[129] It is the stereotypical reason why a woman three decades younger than her rich husband, would be called a gold digger chasing a money bag while waiting for her husband to die. A famous sports player was even said to have gone so far as to place his assets in his mother's name, to avoid his wife taking his wealth through divorce.[130]

Often in modern Western culture, cheating is arguably encouraged, and the society promotes gender mixing in schools and workplaces.[131] Two unsupervised people, can frequently work late at the office on a project together alone. Biological forces, hormones and desires come into play, and before you know it, you may fall in love with your boss. You spend more time with your boss then the few minutes you see your spouse before bed, or as they rush off to work after breakfast. If you want a fruitful marriage, never flirt with anyone other than your partner. As well, do not acknowledge others who will try and flirt with you, whether through social media or in person. However, due to desires and lack of self-control, many often give into flirtations and lust, ultimately poisoning their primary relationship.

The best course of action would be to have a prenuptial marriage contract signed prior to marrying the person you love and want to spend the rest of your life with. If he or she refuses, using excuses such as, "It is as if you are ending the marriage before it begins." Then consider if you are willing to bet half of your life assets based on your feelings of love for them at the time. They may say things such as, "Do you not trust me?" or "You should not marry someone if you do not trust them." Yes, you should marry someone only if you trust them fully. Though understand that most humans can change their mindset and values, and most are easily persuaded by the lies told by others. Are you willing to risk it all when statistics show that almost half of marriages currently end in divorce? It is much easier to have your future partner sign a paper which offers some protection, rather than deal with the stress, time and expense that comes with a divorce. As you never know when one of her guy friends who she thinks of as a brother, will surprise her by revealing his secret desire for her. How many men have lost their wives after their businesses or health took a turn for the worse?

If you are in a marriage, and you do not fully trust your partner, do not have a child thinking that the baby will bring you and your spouse closer. A baby will not fix the marriage. Bringing another human life into this world and taking proper care of them, takes money, time, and love until they are adults. It is a big responsibility. Having a kid in an unhealthy marriage will only make things more complicated. Young children require a lot of attention and can be very stressful to take care of. When you have a child, you will likely be lacking a lot of sleep during the first few years, while having to wake up in the middle of the night to change diapers or feed them. When you are lacking sleep, you may not be as coherent as usual. You may also become more irritable and easily annoyed with your partner. Therefore, ensure you have a drama-free marriage before bringing a child into this world.

Chapter 5: Childhood Trauma

Practically all parents make many minor mistakes when raising their children. However, they are actually trying their best to raise their children, within their financial and intellectual capabilities. Most parents have their child's best interest in their hearts. However, there are a few selfish, immature parents, who can damage a child and leave them traumatized for life. For example, a father may tease his daughter by constantly calling her fat or ugly. She may be beautiful, but still feel that she is ugly due to her father's comments. This can cause her to feel insecure and seek outside validation from unworthy boys at school. They may take advantage of her, and she will give her virginity to the first guy that shows her any attention. She may then become very promiscuous and begin sleeping around with countless men, amounting to a triple digit body count[132] before she completes high school. She may become pregnant, and not be able to complete a high level of education because of this. The parents will blame the child. However, the majority of an adolescent's behaviour is developed from the parents' upbringing of that child. Therefore, we must teach our children good values, and lead by example.

Some parents will not like to hear this, but the fact is that over half of youth in many developed countries have engaged in sexual intercourse before they have completed high school.[133] As well, the way a parent raises their child contributes towards the child's values concerning how they experience sex in life. This goes for the way they respect themselves and the way others will treat them. If you verbally, mentally or physically abuse your child, they will not come to you when they face issues in life. For example, when a girl experiences her first period or if her uncle rapes her, she will not know what to do, and she may not mention it to anyone for years. This is because she is afraid of her parents, and fear is not to be mistaken with respect. Children who come from severely unstable living environments face many difficulties in life, and lose out on many privileges which other children have the opportunity to achieve. The child may not feel confident to enrol in a 4-year university program, out of fear that their parents will get divorced and kick them out of the house prior to completion of their degree program. They will consider that they may not be able to afford the tuition while trying to support themselves.

Parents should be their child's best friend whom they can trust with their secrets. Children will naturally love and respect their parents when they are treated fairly, with kindness and respect. It is still important to discipline your child so that they will learn boundaries when they do something wrong. Parents must explain to their children the reasons why certain behaviours are permitted and others are not. If they spill milk on the carpet, explain to them the cost, time and health issues associated with it. Speak to them respectfully as though they are an adult. Advise them to clean up the mess and assist them by showing them how to clean it up properly. Teach them the reason is so that no mildew will form on the carpet, which may begin to smell bad later. Educate your children to respect other people's property and explain to them how their actions may affect others in life. They will learn to look up to you and respect you as an authoritative figure. However, if you curse at them and beat them, even if they did nothing wrong but simply because you just had a bad day at work, then they will look forward to the day when they can move out.

As a parent, you must control your anger, especially when dealing with fragile children whose emotions are still developing. As well, you must be fair, righteous and noble. Your kids are an investment in life. If you do parenting right, you can be the role model of your child and their friends too. Later in life, they may provide you with excellent retirement opportunities which you were not expecting, to show their gratitude for you.

Many people have children simply out of fulfilment of their desires. They satisfy their sexual urges and desires in the act of sexual intercourse. Or they bring children into this world because procreating is a goal they want to accomplish in life. They may not care to actually have a child to give the child better than what they had themselves. They may not care to raise the child to be healthy, intelligent and athletic. They simply want to check off a box on their bucket list of things to accomplish in their lifetime.

Simply because you conceive a child, does not entitle you the right to abuse and oppress that child, treating them like your slave. Some parents do not care if their child has homework or an important exam to study for. The parents would rather their child do house chores and use them for manual labour. Some parents treat their children as property and feel that they can make all of their child's important life decisions for them, even when the child is an adult. This may include forcing their child to marry someone whom the child is not compatible with and does not want to marry. The way these parents treat their child is a form of oppression, as they sacrifice their child's life and wellbeing for the benefit of themselves.

In the case of failing to allow a boy child to complete his preferred education program, the youngster may grow to be uneducated in life and obtain a low-pay mediocre job. This will inevitably leave the child with significantly fewer women to choose from for marriage. Many decent or successful parents would not want their daughters married to a man whom they do not feel confident in his abilities to provide. As well, the lack of a formal education will affect his status among society and friends, as people will assume that he is unintelligent, and they may try to take advantage of him. This may include his relatives scamming him, or others trying to con him such as through a fake job offer.

This goes the same for parents who slander their child's name. Most parents protect and defend their children, even when their children are at fault or mischievous. However, there are a few psychopath parents who find fun in telling false and demeaning tales about their children to others. These parents may do this for attention, amusement and to make people laugh at their child's expense. What this does, is give relatives permission to take severe advantage over the child. The relatives know that the child's parents will not protect and defend the child. The parents are essentially encouraging others to abuse their own child, sometimes without knowing it. In some cases, these parents are mentally and physically abusive, and they will even hit the child if he or she were to complain of the parents slandering their name.

Some parents speak insultingly of their child to practically everyone they know, which causes the child's relatives and society to look down on the child. This may include a distant cousin raping a girl child, or an aunt running away with the life savings of her nephew. Parents may make up stories, saying that their daughter is very promiscuous. This can cause unwanted advances from perverted or player guys who just want to have sex with her. As well, it can keep away good gentlemen who could have made that girl's dreams come true. Slandering your child's name can lead to cousins, aunts and uncles continuing to slander that child's name with others far and wide in the community. This will potentially prevent them from gaining jobs and getting married.

A son may attend a gathering at a religious place of worship and meet new people he has never met before, only to be treated badly before people even get to know him. He will later discover that some of those in the gathering are friends with his mother, who defamed his character with them behind his back. This will force the child to close himself out from the world and keep distant from his family. He may lock himself up in his bedroom, until he can finally move out of the horrific and sometimes unbearable situation at home, created by his psychopath parents.

Living in such an environment can cause serious mental health issues for the child which can last a lifetime. The child may begin to contemplate suicide as being the only way out of such a situation. These surviving children are the ones who grow up having no issues with moving far away, to get away from the poisonous life which their parents have created for them. Unfortunately, these selfish, narcissistic parents, often get away with tormenting their children in life.

A young child may be put through traumatizing events in their early years, and the parents might not allow that child to express themselves. The child will then hold in their emotional responses, which should not be held inside of them. The parents may curse or hit the child when the child attempts to defend themselves or complain to others about their abusive situation at home. Violent parents have an upper hand on the child, as the child is young with no income, and thus dependent on the adult for life necessities such as food and shelter. The adult is physically much bigger and stronger than the child. Thus, the child is helpless against the abuse.

When a parent continually takes their child's money from a young age, this further deepens the life-lasting effects on the child. It prevents the child from defending themselves, out of fear for losing their money held by the parent. This allows the parent to do virtually whatever abuse they wish to do to that child, forcing the child to simply take it. If the child were to complain, these parents would become more abusive, violent and enraged towards the child for complaining of being abused by them.

In some rare cases, your parents may have even been jealous of you, and they would try to punish you for being decent, honest or successful; especially if your values do not align with their way of life. Both of your parents may have been working and living in a big house. Yet, they would make you go to school with holes in your shoes and with no winter coat in a cold climate. Out of greed, your parents may have demanded your money, though you were just a child. Perhaps they would stop cooking for you, cuss you down and hit you if you refused to give them more of your money. This can cause lifelong scars both mentally and financially, which you may never recover from nor receive full compensation for in life. It is difficult to live your dreams when family controls your life and your money.

Parents should never be biased towards one child over another. If for example, you have a son saving up for his first home as a young boy, do not violently cuss him down almost daily and take his money. Do not use his money to pay for your huge mortgage and buy your daughter a luxury car. These are not his responsibilities and he has his own life to live. He is still a child building himself up, and you are robbing him while taking his life away.

Do not use your son's life savings, to pay for his older sister to go partying away at university for four years, while studying the easiest course. By doing so, you create sibling rivalry and an unfair advantage. You will cause your son to resent you when he grows older, as you may have prevented him from getting married and buying his own house. You will have caused your son to be depressed and live an unfulfilled life, as you prevented him from accomplishing his goals that he has worked hard for. You caused the older daughter to be entitled and spoiled, while you caused irreparable loss of opportunity, emotional damage and strain in your son's life. Whether you want to admit it or not, essentially, you ruined his life.

Some parents are so biased towards one child, they maliciously would not even allow their other child to have something as simple and inexpensive as a chocolate cake for their birthday. Why? Because the favoured child does not like chocolate. They will advise the neglected child that they are selfish for wanting a cake which they desire for their own birthday. Whereas the favoured child is privileged to have their preferred cake on both occasions, their own birthday and on their neglected sibling's birthday. These scenarios are interchangeable between sons and daughters. A parent should never be biased towards one child, regardless of their age or gender. Each child deserves equal and fair opportunities in life.

Unfortunately, in such cases you must accept that your parents are unfair and selfish people who may have ruined your life. Accept that they did not care much for you, nor had your best interests in their hearts. You must learn to cope and manage going through your life the best you can on your own, just as you always have. Avoid thinking about your traumatic experiences every single day of your adult life, as this can cause you to fall into deep depression. Consider your life experience and ponder on things you can excel at while you move forward. Unfortunately, you were too obedient, kind and respectful to your family, when most other children were unmannerly and defiant. You may have been little, quiet or weak, and your parents took advantage of this. Not much could be done to change things with violent, ignorant and stubborn parents. This life is not always fair.

These traumatic events can cause a person to turn to drugs, alcohol or other addictive intoxicants, in order to drown out the pain caused by their parents.[134] These coping mechanisms can continue into the child's adulthood, and have an unhealthy impact on their body and mind; such as the development of cardiovascular and liver disease.[135] Thinking about things that you went through as a child, can also have a lasting mental effect, such as crying during movies when you see a loving family scene, because you never experienced that love from your own family in life. It can cause a person to jump from relationship to relationship seeking affection, and have that person be used and abused by society. When a child is constantly cussed down and yelled at in childhood, they feel as though they are never good enough. Especially when they did nothing wrong. They develop personality traits such as becoming a perfectionist or a people pleaser, being very nice to everyone they meet. Consequently, they will not know how to tell a person "No," when that person crosses their boundaries.

When your parents beat you and yell at you for things you did not do, it can have a devastating impact on your mental health in adulthood. Such as when your younger sibling breaks a vase or runs away with the family car which you had nothing to do with. Or when your parents curse at you on a regular basis, and use violence to prevent you from saying anything about it. You will grow up having other people in life take advantage of you also. You will feel that you are not allowed to express yourself nor tell people how you feel, out of fear of upsetting people. So, you will become a pushover in life. People will potentially take advantage of you sexually, physically, financially or use you for your time and energy. You will fully realize that they are taking advantage of you, and be afraid to tell them "No," because you were not allowed to refuse your parents ever.

You will have daily stresses from people build up inside of you, until one day you may explode on one unfortunate soul. You may also have insomnia caused by overthinking, as well as develop a pessimistic outlook on life, as you will always be expecting and preparing for the worst-case scenario. This is because your parents were always in a bad mood, getting very upset over little and unimaginable things. The stresses you faced in childhood can cause you to develop health issues, and you may even become more susceptible to having a heart attack or dementia.[136]

Some immigrant parents from developing countries, are expressively and excessively abusive when raising their children. No matter how hard the kid tries to be perfect and obedient while trying to please their parents, the parents would still curse and hit the child, telling their child that he or she is not good enough. The child would do whatever their parents would ask of them and do a good job. Yet, their parents would always make up faults or accuse the child of not performing the task well. This child will grow up not loving themselves, and this can continue until they die. They will be used by people as they will always say yes when asked by anyone to do almost anything.

This child will grow up with built-up anger in them, which may come out in their actions such as driving very aggressively. They may play very rough and aggressive in sports, or do activities which many may view as potentially dangerous and extreme. This person will not value their wellbeing nor the safety of their life the way most people do. These actions and behaviours can be traced back to the parents' upbringing of the child, which has caused them to live in such a manner. They were not allowed to express themselves, nor refuse to do something within their rights while growing up. Unfortunately, some of us were raised by psychopathic, narcissist, selfish parents. We must overcome this trauma so we can stand up for ourselves when dealing with others. This will allow us to live a peaceful and more fulfilled life.

In order to move past childhood trauma, we must acknowledge that our parents were not fair, and lacked better moral judgment to no fault of our own. We must acknowledge that our parents were either physically, mentally or financially abusive; or a combination of all three, and we did not deserve that. We must learn to appreciate ourselves for our skills and values, which make us unique and great in society. Some of us may be great at a certain sport, or great at cooking or writing. We may have hidden talents which we previously were afraid to unleash and shine in for the world. We must learn to love and be kind to ourselves, the way we are often kind to others, despite what negative traits and lies our family may say about us.

Many serial killers and psychopaths went through severe childhood trauma in their lives, and although they have no right to kill an innocent person as a result, their parents should be held partially accountable for their actions in society.[137] However, all the blame falls on the murderer, regardless of their past upbringing which made them that way. Without addressing the parents' behaviour and poor judgment in how they raised their child, and without any serious penalties and consequences, parents will continue to severely abuse their children, and more serial killers will be made.

These made serial killers, should be sent to therapy and counselling, to learn how to live a normal life and reintegrate into society. They should be educated to become healthy functioning adults, who can express themselves and stand up for themselves, in a typical, normal, and acceptable manner in society. When you call these people monsters, it only further teaches them that they are unwanted and that something is wrong with them, as though they are not allowed to defend themselves. They often did not stand up for themselves when being bullied in school or taken advantage of by co-workers. Until they finally, excessively defended themselves using violence. We must understand what they went through which made them that way, and not take advantage of abused children who grew up and are trying to live normal lives. We must teach them how to respond and react in a normal fashion, before it gets to the point where they can no longer take any more abuse from others.

When you have been through a childhood of excessive traumatic experiences caused by your parents, it is best to try and become independent of them and focus on your future. Do not allow your parents to ruin your adult life the way they stole your childhood away from you. If they are a threat and danger to your health, life, career or marriage, isolate the toxic habits they try to impose on you, so that you can live a more peaceful, prosperous and healthy life.

You grew up to be a very independent person. You need to gain the self-confidence to trust yourself in making your own life decisions, without hearing a voice in your head telling you that you cannot do it. You are likely more intelligent at problem solving and innovative thinking than the majority of people around you. However, you lack the self-confidence that other people possess, even though you may be better at a certain task. Believe in yourself and take control of your life. Set goals and keep a backup plan, as you may not have family to fall back on if you fail in life.

Learn to take calculated risks in things you believe in, such as investing, buying that property you saved up for and taking on that course you are afraid of failing. If you think you can do it, you may likely be able to do it better than most others can. Once you can get over your childhood trauma, you may even consider going into a decision-making career such as politics. This can be a profession you will likely flourish in better than most who lack your upbringing. A career in politics or upper management can demonstrate to others that you are responsible, hard-working and a very fair person who considers others when making decisions. Rise to the life that you deserve, and do not let toxic, violent parents bring you down. Do your moves in private until you succeed.

The way we raise our children, has an everlasting impact on their values, character and their associated fears and habits in life. If a child is raised in a home of alcohol abuse and violence, this will reflect on the child's future. They may continue the trend and become abusive alcoholics themselves. Or they may break free and use the torment as motivation, striving to become a doctor or working with a non-profit organization, improving the lives of others who have faced similar trauma.

If you come from parents who yell at you for things you did not do growing up, you will constantly overthink things, and will be always afraid of being blamed or getting yelled at for things which are not your fault. For example, you might be afraid to ask your boss for your entitled time off to attend a funeral for a loved one, as you may think that your boss will yell at you for asking. This fear will also be apparent in the way you behave with friends, roommates and relatives. Try to build your confidence and realize that not everyone will yell at you in life for things you have no control over, or things that are not your fault. Otherwise, you will continue being afraid to stand up for yourself, and never do things in your life such as starting a business or asking your crush out on a date.

Generally, parents are physically bigger than their young children, and have physical control over them. Some parents violently abuse their children, throwing them against the walls, slapping them, and beating them with items ranging from pot spoons, belts, shoes and pans. One parent may have issues with their in-laws and take their anger out on their child. These children become accustomed to the normality in their lives of being abused, often for things they may have no control over. These children often develop mental health issues, such as depression and anxiety, which can have life-long lasting negative effects.[138]

These children often feel that if they were to complain to the authorities, they would not receive adequate long-term assistance. Often, they may be just taken for a few hours, examined, then sent right back to their abusive parents again. This would only infuriate the parents more, so the parents would take their anger out on the child and teach their child not to complain about the abuse. This leads to children growing up as hyper-independent, withdrawn from society and experiencing a hard time making friends. They may live in sorrow and loneliness, which makes it hard for them to feel motivated to do anything progressive with themselves. These children have parents who made them feel worthless as an individual growing up, and it has caused their brains to develop in a way which is not a healthy or normal way for a human to live in society.

As an adult, when dealing with the majority of people within a fast-paced metropolis, you will need to be stern, a bit loud, and assertive to get your point across and heard. This is especially important in certain Western societies, where talking loudly and raising voices in arguments is acceptable. When confronting people, do not be shy and timid, as this can show weakness for the other person to exploit. However, if you are speaking with another humble and timid individual, there is no need to be very assertive. They will likely appreciate the kind, soft request from you, rather than an aggressive shock. Perhaps they have experienced some trauma of their own. As well, there are some beautiful cultures in the world such as Japan, where humbling yourself is not only the norm, but a sign of respect.[139] In such cases, assimilate yourself to the culture and enjoy the peaceful nature of the people.

If you hate doing a certain task, and you feel as though you are being used when doing something for a person, speak up about it. Do not continue to do the task because this is the way you were raised. If you do not complain, then your boss will continue giving you more work than your co-workers, and family will continue using you. Whether it is your boss, friend or family member, it is important to voice your concerns and make them understand the negative impact that their abuse is having on your life. They may use you without realizing any long-term effects, such as loss of your sleep, depriving you from spending time to help your dependents or tending to other personal matters. You may be prepared for the worst when you confront a person, such as thinking that they might hit you. However, stand up for yourself, as you may be surprised to see they likely will not even yell at you, nor hit you as you might expect. So, stop being Mrs./Mr. Too Nice!

It is not your fault for living your life in fear of others. Ideally, parents should be educated on the causes and effects of their actions and punished for oppressing their children. However, this life is far from perfect and not fair. Often times, kids who go through childhood trauma will have difficulty trusting people. In situations of child abuse, it may be helpful to try and secretly save your money from a young age. Then escape from your parents' home when you have a good financial foundation, and when you are legally able to start your life and become independent. You may also wish to seek assistance from a trustworthy person capable, willing and responsible enough to take care of you. This may be a teacher or relative such as an aunt or uncle, who will not just quit on you and tell your parents that you suggested the idea.

Some countries have organizations which relocate abused children to other households, with strangers who are willing to adopt the child and take care of them.[140] You will need to do research on the country you reside in to understand what the process is. As well, confirm what obligations you would need to meet for this program to help you. It would be a big step, but may be better than enduring more years of suffering at the hands of selfish parents. These parents may also have anger management issues and do not want to admit that they have a problem. Some parents may verbally tell you they love you, but take their anger out on you because their mortgage is stressing them out. Therefore, it may be better to leave as soon as you safely can, by contacting a trusted relative, friend, or the authorities if you are willing to go that route.

If you grew up in a home without being loved, you may find it hard to love your parents. As a result, you may grow up loving material things such as luxury vehicles. You may also fall in love easily, even if it is with a person who is bad for you. You will be starving for love from others and wanting to give love too. However, this can lead to you not being able to judge the bad intention of others, and you may fall into their traps. They could have the intention to take advantage of you and use you for sex or steal your money.

When parents yell at their kids and do not give them family support, the kids grow up being afraid to do things in life, because they will be afraid of getting in trouble, or afraid of downfall and becoming homeless. Excessively abusive parents may punish and control their children undeservingly, by using violence towards the child if they do not comply with what is demanded of them. This can create youth who are fearful to lead and afraid to take chances in life. They become followers with timid character, who are easily manipulated by others. People will order them around and expect them to be very agreeable, treating them as slaves the way their parents treated them. These youth are always afraid of being yelled at or hit, so they do not want to stand up for their dignity and basic human rights. If these innocent souls would get over their fear, or are given a chance to be in charge of a big project, they may be the best of leaders. They can be very efficient, fair and reliable, ensuring that the job gets done correctly and on time.

Selfish, violent and unfair parents can create hyper-independent, perfectionist children, who do not have much fun in life. These children can be excellent problem solvers and intelligent, but regarded by some as selfish. They may value material things more than others. These children may become independent in life from a young age, because they feel as though they did not have anyone to turn to or back them up when they faced problems. Depending on their upbringing, children who are from households of highly unfair and abusive families, may become more serious-minded, shy and objective in adulthood. They will prefer to do things on their own because they have been lied to and disappointed by countless people previously in life.

If your parents were extremely abusive and unjust towards you in your childhood, ensure that you have the ability to maintain independence from them. Make your own decisions moving forward in your life, and ensure that you safeguard your current and future life from their negativity. You may choose to continue maintaining ties with them due to the relationship status of them being your parents. Also, many cultures and religions emphasize the importance of showing respect and kindness to one's parents. However, that does not give them any right to trample all over your rights as a human being.

Analyze and accept what happened, and do not beat yourself up over their mistakes. Move forward in your adult life on your own, independent from their violence, abuse and slander as best as you can. In some cases, one parent may have experienced stress from their in laws or just had a bad sex life, and wrongfully took their anger out on you. Perhaps later on your parents will get divorced. After they are apart and reach old age, they will realize their faults and reconciliation may be possible to mend your relationship with them.

Chapter 6: Money

Money is one of the most stressful things many of us will deal with in life. The majority of mankind desires money, property, status, sex and fame. Not all of these are desired by everyone. But money is something that the vast majority of people desire, and it relates to all of these things. You want status? Often money gets you that or comes from that. You want a pretty wife? Money can get you that too. There is nothing wrong with wanting to be rich. The problem is that many people are greedy, and they want to become rich by cheating others.

Whether it be your abusive father taking your money since you were seven years old. Or politicians swindling taxpayer dollars for their luxurious lifestyle, while ordinary citizens are forced to work extra hours to fund it.[141] People wracking havoc on your finances can cause you to fall into depression, get terminally ill and become suicidal. You may do business with someone, and they commit fraud and rob you of hundreds of thousands of dollars. You may even want to kill the person responsible, while outsiders unaware of the circumstances will label you as psychotic and mentally ill. In reality, you may in fact be mentally unstable as a result of the stress caused by the actions of others. Health and wealth are very important in life. Do not listen to people who tell you money is evil. If they did not need money, then they would not work and they should be happy living as homeless bums. Yet they get up and go to work, and may ask you to "borrow" money to fund their excessive lifestyle.

In contrast, there are people who may be considered cheap. People who are very frugal with their money do not necessarily enjoy their stingy spending habits. They are cost-conscious out of either fear or determination. We must know what cheap people value in life to understand how they think and what their concerns are. Some may be very frugal out of fear of living on the streets if they were to lose their job. Most people have their families whom they can depend on should they lose all their money, and many take this for granted without even considering it. Thus, most will spend and enjoy their lives, subconsciously knowing that they have someone that will support them in dire circumstances. Some cheap people do not have family to depend on in their lives. They grew up very independently and understood the value of money from a young age. They saved their money for a rainy day and may not ever ask to borrow money from others. If they should lose their job, they are in a far better situation financially than most.

Some men are cheap throughout their youth because they are saving for marriage, and they wish to live a stable, modest life and retire early. Other so called cheap people, save their money with an end goal. They may want to buy a house and have a nice car. So, they will work hard, saving their money until they accomplish their goals in life. Once they have their house paid off and accomplish their other financial goals, they may transform into a very freely spending person, enjoying their best life.

Some young people say, they do not save for the future because they can make money later, but they will never be in their twenties while backpacking through Europe again. Others may say, they can travel with their partner in their forties, but they will never be able to pay off for a rental property in their twenties again. This rental property can potentially generate a supplementary income for their day job. The choice of enjoying life when you are young or working hard and saving for the future is up to you. There is no definitive right or wrong answer. It is simply a lifestyle decision you make once you truly understand what you want in life. Regardless of our choices, we should also respect the decision of others in their own lives.

Many people who save and accumulate their wealth become the target of people within their circle. The first step you should take to protect yourself from being robbed is to never reveal your true financial status to anyone. Not your siblings, not your aunt that you trust so much, and definitely not your co-workers or business partners. Friends, family, and even strangers will always be jealous of the possessions you worked hard for, which they are not willing to make the same sacrifices to achieve themselves. They will want to use your money so that they can easily thrive, while putting you further behind in life after your previous struggles to get to where you are. People are generally selfish, inconsiderate individuals, who will lie, cheat, and take your money if they think they can easily get away with it.

If you wish to live a peaceful life, it requires restraint, until you reach a status high enough that you are able to easily protect yourself and your wealth. Once you reach a certain level, you should be able to afford top lawyers and additional security measures. However, if you are simply upper-middle class or in the process of building your empire, then keep striving while maintaining a low profile.

Enjoy your wealth, and let your spouse and kids treat you like their superhero. No need to advertise on social media nor flaunt your wealth for others to be envious. They can scheme of ways to deceive and cheat you out of your wealth. Be low key and restrain yourself from showing off. No need for paparazzi to chase you taking away your privacy. Consider dressing in normal casual clothes instead of designer brands, even if you can afford expensive stuff. Afterall, who are we trying to impress when we can live a peaceful life under the radar? If you work in a sales profession, a reasonably nice watch and modest luxury car can help boost the image of yourself and your company. This would be an exception, as you may need to invest some money in your business to gain new clients.

It is unfortunate that the poor money management skills of others may have a negative impact on the lives of us all. Most adults in developed countries have the financial mindset of a spoiled child. Whether they are adults with children, or elected prime ministers and presidents, this attitude seems the same. They were often born into privileged families, where they never experienced famine or hardship in life. They were accustomed to getting what they want as a child and grew older, never learning the value of hard work to earn their own way in life. They were dependent on their parents' wealth, then some untruthfully state that their wealth was self-made.

Money management and financial literacy is seldom taught in many public education systems. When a typical teenager receives their first paycheck, instead of saving it and spending on the bare essentials, they often invite a friend to the mall to see what they can spend it on. Brand name athletic shoes, fancy dining and entertainment at a young age, while their parents provide food, clothing and shelter. However, this is an opportunity that will never return in life for many. As you read this book, it is probably too late for most to go back in the past and take advantage of your years when you were living at home rent-free.

As an adolescent, you can push yourself hard and save the most for a foundation that can set your future ahead of the majority of your peers. Some even go through life, only using a loan for their university education and their first home. If you do take a student loan to pay for your degree, make sure it is a program that will yield a high paying salary in a high demand career. Consider if it will likely be a stable job, where you have the security of not being let go easily during hard times, such as in a pandemic or recession. Consider new trends in the world such as artificial intelligence, which may make your position obsolete depending on your career choice. Alternatively, you can consider an apprenticeship, such as to become an electrician, plumber or a mechanic. These jobs often pay you part-time while you are working throughout your school program. As the baby boomers and elder generation retire and die off, there will be more demand for hands-on jobs which pay reasonably well. It is something worth considering.

For those who are still teenagers or living at home with their parents, I urge you to take advantage of your childhood. Work hard and save. Do not splurge on high-priced clothing, or expensive outings with friends who you will not keep in touch with in your adulthood. A lot of times friends do not care about your wellbeing. They simply want to have fun in life. Many people are not satisfied in their own lives, and waste money buying junk for short bursts of dopamine to feel happy temporarily. They do not often know what they truly want in life, and are envious of others, wanting what other people have. If you buy a particular model of vehicle, they may unoriginally strive to buy the same model of car.

Nevertheless, most people do not want to make sacrifices and work hard to achieve success in life. Yet, they become upset and jealous with others who put in the time, effort and work. Many people try and take shortcuts in life and cheat others to build wealth. Therefore, you must use tremendous caution when dealing with people, as many will do sneaky, violent, and dishonest things for money. Most people will be jealous of your wealth and high status, even when they say they are happy for you.

Occasionally, celebrities who quickly rise to fame or people who win the lottery do not know how to responsibly manage their newfound wealth. As a result, many end up broke or hooked on drugs, while they splurge on everything they can think of in their hopeless pursuit of happiness. Do not give into societal norms, or peer pressure to purchase the latest smartphone when your current one is working well. Do not feel that because you do not have the current and latest gadget, it will deem you as uncool. In decades to follow, when you can pay off your primary home and two rental income properties, all will see who the real cool person is. The real cool and smart person is the one who showed restraint in their youth, while others were busy keeping up appearances among their peers. As well, those who did not struggle in life by working hard for what they have from a young age, will not appreciate things given to them without any effort.

There is nothing wrong with saving the environment and saving money, by wearing clothes for more than two years, and driving an economy car for two decades until it no longer runs. Choosing a car is an important decision, and it may be the second most expensive purchase you will make in life.[142] A car is a personal choice, and often stimulates emotions and adornment from its owner. Choose a car that is reliable, safe, fuel efficient and which you find pleasing to look at and drive. Whether the fuel be gasoline, hydrogen or electricity, ensure that it is efficient in its consumption. After a decade, if your car is still reliable and fuel efficient, you will be more inclined to keep it and spend money on necessary maintenance. Especially if you still find it attractive and fun to drive.

Dependability is important, because having an unreliable car can be a stressful experience. There will be many people including women who will judge a man based on materialistic things such as the clothes he wears and the car he drives. If you are a man, should you care? Well, that depends on your priorities. Do you want to enjoy your youth building temporary social connections and fun memories? Or would you prefer to work hard, and potentially retire early with a trophy wife and luxury cars. Try to avoid financing things in your youth which you can pay for in cash. A good strategy for a peaceful life, is to build wealth and not accumulate debt. You can always buy a second-hand, but still reliable car that can get you through your hustling years while you build your empire.

When you are buying a luxury product such as a high-end latte from your favourite café, ask yourself if you want it, or if you are simply buying into the hype and marketing surrounding that product. Is it truly superior to the cheaper competitor's coffee? Does it use sustainably sourced beans and taste better? Or do you just want to take a selfie to post on social media and show off? If someone were to ask you why you paid much more for a luxury item such as a bag or a watch, can you rationally explain what makes that product better? Or are you just paying for the logo?

When you make big purchases, such as a new television or an oven, try and buy something of good quality that will last a long time. It may not be the cheapest option upfront. But it is cheaper to buy something of high quality that will last many years, rather than buying the same item many times over after the previous item breaks. However, also bear in mind that many products today are intentionally designed to fail or become obsolete after a predetermined timeframe or once the warranty is over. This is for corporations to ensure that consumers will continually spend money to buy new products throughout their lifespan.[143] This causes more pollution through manufacturing, and causes more environmental damage as it creates more waste through the disposal of products. If your fridge lasted twenty-five years instead of five years, then the manufacturers would be losing a lot of money from potential new sales. Therefore, you do not need to buy the fanciest and most expensive fridge or television, because it may not last more than a few years anyway. This can save you some stress later, by not feeling distraught over wasting $10,000 on an 8K high-definition television, that dies before you get to watch any 8K programming on it.

It is unfortunate that many companies purposely engineer their products to fail, so that consumers are stuck in a cycle of purchasing new products every few years. Whether it be on a corporate scale or an individual level, the majority of people are dishonest. This is not politically correct, but this is the reality. Many people lie to their partner, friends or boss on a daily basis, and consider their dishonesty to be harmless white lies.[144] Imagine if someone left you with one million dollars cash in a bag and asked you to keep it safe for them for twenty years. Would you use some of that money for yourself? Such as occasionally taking some money for food delivery or unexpected vehicle repairs. It is not your money, it is someone else's money entrusted to you, which you are responsible for. Yet, most people would not hesitate to use some or all of the money if given the chance. An honest person would not even want the responsibility to hold someone else's money or belongings, as that would be an added stress to worry about, such as ensuring that no one else steals it. Most people are selfish. Again, this is not politically correct, but it is true. It is something you must come to reality with, and keep in mind throughout your daily interactions with people.

You can tell a lot about a person's character, decency and honesty based on how often they ask you for favours or money. A truly honest person with integrity and good character will strive for true independence. They would rather struggle with a job on their own, taking forty hours to build a fence, rather than bother someone else for assistance which can cut the time in half. They are always considerate of others, and they would rather go hungry rather than disturb someone by asking them to borrow money. A truly upright individual with excellent character, would ponder if they will live long enough to repay any money they may borrow from another person. As you never know when your time to die will be, and you may die before you are able to repay your debts.

A dishonest person may borrow money from everyone they can, and often say things such as, "Can you buy me lunch? I'll pay you back." However, whether small or large amounts of money, they make no note of money used from others, and have no intention of ever re-paying you. Instead, they will hope that you will forget about it. Often the person who is owed the money may feel shy or ashamed to ask for it. So, their silence is taken by the debtor as indication that the loan was forgotten. In reality, it may bother that person who is owed money, and they may even feel stressed and lose sleep thinking about it.

When people have your money, they have control over you and your life, or at least to a certain degree. Instead of being able to live independently, you may be forced to rely on this same person who owes you money or depend on other people in life. You may need a place to stay, or request rides from people, as you do not have your own money in your possession to purchase your own home and vehicle. You will be forced to be nice to that person that owes you money, when you feel like being mean, because they are refusing to give you back your money. People may take a significant amount of something from you such as money or property. Then in their defence, they will mention some minor favour they did for you, which was not nearly as valuable as what they took from you.

A person may have stolen your trust fund and used it when you were younger. Then they would say "Well, remember those few times I cooked for you, I treated you like my own child the month that you stayed with me, so it's not a big deal that I used $100,000 of your trust fund money." Clarify sternly that their action of robbing you was not authorized by you in any way. As well, educate them on the dollar value equation, as to the vast difference in what they took, compared to the unsubstantial favour they did for you. Educate them on the circumstances and impact that their actions have had on your life. For example, if you were forced to live with them because they had control over your money. Advise them that you needed your money to buy your own home, but now thanks to their actions, you cannot.

If they persist in bypassing you, and pretend as though they did you a favour when you confront them about the money which they stole from you, then ask them sternly to allow you the opportunity to do the same thing to them. Tell them to give you $100,000 and let them eat a few meals cooked by you in exchange. They will likely become infuriated at you even suggesting such an idea. Yet, they did it to you and see nothing wrong in it. Take them to court. Or deal with them however which way you can, while maintaining the boundaries of the law, and basic morally accepted principles.

Do not be afraid of taking someone to court when you have done nothing wrong. Typically, lawyers can be very expensive. If you cannot afford a good lawyer, you can study the laws in your region related to the problem you are facing. This way, you can represent yourself in court with facts and evidence. You may watch television court shows for your country as well, which can help familiarize yourself with the process and what to expect. This can be helpful in future potential cases you may face as well.

Be careful of those who tell you that they will not cheat you simply because they are already rich. Many people in business become wealthy by cheating their customers. These are often the ones who are very inconsiderate, selfish, and will continue cheating others out of their money until they die. No matter how much they have, they will always feel as though they do not have enough. Many people in sales will use pressure tactics and deceit, to convince you to commit to something you do not feel comfortable doing. They may show you fake text messages stating that the item is in high demand from other people.

Stand firm by being assertive with them and tell them you need time to think about it. Or simply reply to them saying "No." Some people may say in these situations, they need to consult with their spouse prior to making such a decision. What I usually do, is call them out and tell them, if their product is so superior, then they would not need to pressure me into signing up for it without time to think about it. I tell them, if their product is so great and in high demand, I should be the one begging them to give me the opportunity to purchase the product, instead of them pressuring me. If you are a physically small or weak person, consider taking along a friend with a bigger stature to avoid being intimidated or taken advantage of. Do not fall for pyramid schemes and upfront membership fees for programs you will not use.

When people scam you or steal your money, the laws in some Western countries protect criminals, even though you are the victim.[145] Therefore, you must focus and exercise self-control. Ensure that you do not have any private interactions, where they can falsify a story and say that you threatened them or became violent with them. This will give them the upper hand if the police and justice system believe their lies. You could even be charged or put in jail for something you did not do. Ensure you have all in-person interactions recorded on hidden camera or microphone if permitted in your country. As well, have several witnesses if possible. You can also communicate through text messages or email and keep records of all conversations to prove your innocence if needed later. Finally, have them admit to the money they owe you or whatever crime they may have committed against you. Sue them and put a lien on their property after successful court proceedings.

To avoid dishonest people from taking advantage of you, be stern with them from the start. Give them an excuse as to why you cannot lend them money and cannot buy them lunch. Eventually, they may learn not to ask you anymore. If they are not qualified for a loan from the bank, then it may be a good indication that they will likely not be a good candidate to lend money to. If you are not in a good financial situation yourself, it may be best to avoid lending money to people at all.

It is not selfish to avoid bailing people out of their stupid mistakes. If they blew their paycheck on parties and concerts, and now they need money for rent, let them learn the hard way. It may help them become responsible in the future. If they do not punish and learn from their mistakes in life, they will often continue depending on others to bail them out. It is good practice even when dealing with family members or close friends, to always get things signed in writing. This includes when you lend things out which are of significant value to you. A good rule to follow, is to never let anyone borrow something that you want to have returned to you. If you have a special edition chrome tool set which you love, do not lend it out to people. If it is a good friend, you can offer to help them fix whatever they need to use it for as an alternative. Be stern and tell them straight, "I do not lend out my tools" or whatever it is that they are asking to borrow.

Many people are irresponsible from a young age, then request to utilize your resources for their benefit, after you did the responsible thing and planned long-term for your life. It is often the "cool" troublesome kids in high school, who end up flipping burgers in their twenties. It is often the girls who sell themselves online in their youth, who will regret it in their adulthood when it is too late to go back.

Currently, there is a trend with some women striving to become millionaires by hosting online sex streaming services, where men pay a subscription fee to view or interact with them. These independent women can become financially free and pay off a house at an early age. Yet, when their prime years of beauty fade away in their late twenties and they want to have a family, their erotic professional history may deem them as unsuitable for the criteria of many men. Afterall, not many men want to walk in public with "their" girl, knowing that thousands of other guys have seen the most intimate parts of their wife's body. Although Selling sex for money can yield a substantial amount of cashflow, this comes at the risk of sexually transmitted diseases, unwanted pregnancy, potential violence, and the reputation of your public image. This can also diminish your future career prospects.

When making money, there are sometimes ways to profit from timing, such as with cryptocurrency or stocks. However, you may need a decent amount of capital to invest in certain options. As well, there is a risk that you can lose much of your initial investment. I do not recommend these options if you are not familiar with cryptocurrency and stocks.

Always think long-term when making money and consider how the ways you make money may impact your future. If you own a business, will you cheat your customers and risk someone coming after your children? Will you steal from a business owner and risk going to jail? You need to consider the consequences, prior to committing any unjust acts to cheat others. Moreover, you must protect yourself from others who will try to steal your wealth. For some, this life is a game, and they live as though they will not be held accountable for their actions committed outside of the law. If they can commit a heinous crime, and rob an innocent soul for some monetary gain, they will complete the criminal action without hesitation. They will not consider the devastating harm caused to their victim.

When your hire a professional to complete a job for you such as home renovations, do not pay the full amount upfront before the work is completed. Instead, give a small deposit if required, then pay a little bit at a time until the job is complete. When the work is done as per the agreement, promptly pay any remaining balance owed. If you pay the full amount upfront and they have other clients with jobs waiting, they may run away with your money before they complete your renovation job.[146] With contractors especially, it may also be difficult to track them down after.

It is critical that we understand human nature, desires, and the fact that laws are often all which prevent many people from harming others and stealing their money. People are often controlled by their emotions, greed, lusts and desperation. When a person loses their job, family and health, they may feel as though they have nothing left to lose. This person may become desperate, and willing to take risks which they previously would have not considered. People turn to violence when society crumbles and the cost of living becomes too high. In such scenarios, it is important that we take measures to protect ourselves and retool our skillsets, to ensure good financial stability so we can thrive.

Chapter 7: Cure

So, you've been wronged in life. What now? You may have experienced more stress and trauma in life than most people and now find it hard to fit into society. You may seem weird in social gatherings, and people may not understand your way of thinking or doing things. You may find yourself rarely, or never smiling in photos. At times, you may find much peace in being alone with your thoughts and away from others.

Because people do not understand you or your way of doing things, they will isolate you, which can cause you to fall deeper into depression. You need social stimulation to overcome your depression, but you will lack it increasingly more while people exclude you from social activities due to misunderstanding you. Do not worry about how people disregard you this way. These people have not gone through your journey and trauma, so few will understand. Your way of thinking makes you unique. You might have been forced to deal with your trauma on your own without anyone to pull you out. This has made you hyper-independent and unique from most others in thought process. You can possess the capabilities to uplift others and help solve problems in society and on a global scale, as most do not have the same strength and resilience that you were forced to adopt. Do not give up hope in life. Your time to thrive in life may come when you least expect it.

When you are wronged by someone you have choices. You can merely let it go, like a big poop built up inside of you waiting to drop. This can save you time, as well as your mental and physical energy by removing yourself from the situation and moving forward without compensation. Otherwise, you can confront the person, and attempt to resolve things amicably. This may work if they are a reasonable, calm and logical person. Alternatively, you can take action such as filing a police report and taking them to court.

In several developed nations, you can take a person to court for various reasons, including defamation of character which may be difficult to prove, loss of property, as well as opportunity cost. Again, these options will take time, energy and money, along with being a stressful process. If it will cost you more inconvenience and money than what the person stole from you, it is often better to cut your losses and leave it be, as difficult as that may be to do.

For things that are significantly life impacting, there is often no peace for a person until justice is served. Therefore, make the effort to defend yourself, be assertive, and stand up for your rights in a non-violent way when you can. However, in drastic circumstances such as if your life is in danger, fighting back physically may be your only hope to survive the situation without bodily harm or death. Thus, it is important to seek and maintain the best physical health you can, so that you can have quick reflexes and a healthy body which can withstand impacts. Keeping healthy physically will contribute to achieving good mental health.[147]

What separates alpha males from beta males are money and muscles. Take those things away from the alpha male and you will notice that he will quickly humble himself when he becomes weak, poor, and dependent on others. Do not be intimidated by these tall, muscular, alpha types who speak loudly and talk over other people for attention. With money, a man can buy assets to take advantage of others and become superior to other men. He can buy a house, a big luxury vehicle which gives him presence, and a gym membership. Genetic superiority, and a strong network of friends and family can also assist in this superiority, and many times these friends are drawn to wealth.

Strive to become capable of physically defending yourself. If you are genetically a weaker individual, upgrade your diet and hit the gym to bulk up so that you can protect yourself and your family. Women are naturally drawn to taller and physically stronger men. They seek provision and protection the same way that men seek beauty. Your parents, relatives, friends and society will respect and judge you based on your status and the material possessions you attain in life. You may be treated like a kid until you get married, at which time they will finally consider you as an adult. If you purchase a house, they will further show respect towards you. The same applies to if you have a thriving business or multiple rental properties.

If you cannot protect yourself physically, people will continue to take advantage of you in life, especially if you also lack the intellect and wealth to safeguard yourself. Follow the news and keep up to date with the latest developments in the world. Learn about health and science. Become the most educated and physically best version of yourself possible. Study the legal system in your country, specifically with property, self-defence rights and whatever other issues you may face. This way, even if you need to defend yourself in court, you will be able to stand a chance.

When it comes to defending yourself, different situations require different methods of engagement. We all face a multitude of challenges imposed on us by other individuals. You get to choose what things would be a waste of your energy, and what things you feel would be worth your time, effort, resources and brain cells to fight back against. How do you know which things are worth fighting over and which are best to let go? That is up to you. But, if it will not have a significant negative impact on your financial status, wellbeing, health, and societal reputation in the next two to five years, then it may be best to let it go. However, if you can deal with it swiftly and efficiently, then take care of your business, and let them face the repercussions of their actions, in a legal manner.

If you do try to let it go, then let it go fully and free your mind. Do not waste your time harboring bad energy by thinking about it. Focus on working towards your future, and rebuild better than that which was taken from you. Learn from your mistakes so you do not trust the wrong people again, and keep those dishonest cheaters out of your life. Listen to your intuition and use your best judgement. As well, always get things signed in writing.

Your mind will become weak if you focus on the negative and do not look at the positive in life. Find things that give you peace in your life. This could be taking a walk in the park, reading a book, or doing something that gives you an adrenaline rush. Avoid stressful things that take away your peace. Do not even think about the stressful trauma in your past. You may have many days when you just want to lay in bed crying or sleeping. Do not do this as you are wasting your life. Get your butt out of bed and do something productive such as exercising or getting your laundry done. To prevent yourself from being isolated and overthinking, try to be more social. Dress nicely and take a stroll through a mall, even if you only interact with the store employee while you purchase a product. Try and speak to at least one other human being every day of your life. This will help maintain good mental stimulation.

Look at your world around you, if you do not like it, can you change it? Break free of what is holding you back. If you are obese, go running as hard and often as you can and adjust your diet. Your body is resilient, so take good care of it and do not feel hopeless. Begin gradually working out and then progress to more intense training. Maintaining optimal weight can help protect you from disease. If money is a problem, as it is for many, try to start a side hustle for some added income. Think of your strengths and contemplate ways in which you can capitalize and make money from your talents. Do not be afraid of failure, but always have a backup plan in life.

Try to go outside for fresh air every day or open a window if you cannot go out. Sunlight can also help your recovery process and improve your wellbeing, so consider sunning when you can.[148] These little things in your daily lifestyle can improve your physical and mental health. Your body can feel more energized, and your brain can become more alert, focused and sharper at solving future problems that you will face in life. If you do not have anyone to assist you in life, you need to take care of yourself so that you can be healthy, strong and wise to avoid being taken advantage of. People will try to exploit your weaknesses, and often no one really cares when you are gone. Your employer will replace you, your spouse may remarry and your children will continue their happy lives without you. Therefore, make your life the best it can be for yourself, and take care of your mental and physical health first.

Give priority to important people in your life such as your partner, children and parents. As well, take care of important things in your life such as your health, career, wealth, vehicles and your home. Maintaining these important things will help you be productive and more capable of helping others around you. When you are healthy, strong and wealthy, you will be in a better position to protect and provide for your family, friends and the less fortunate. Do not stress over things that you cannot change. Stay calm and patient waiting for the outcome, then deal with it after you can assess the result. It may be nothing to even worry or stress over.

Help the poor by volunteering at a homeless shelter or tutoring an underprivileged kid. Volunteering is a great way to meet people, which can help boost your mood while you improve the lives of others. Spend your time unwinding in nature, or just sitting on the couch watching a movie after a long day of grinding. Find peace in nature bonding activities, such as canoeing and hiking. The way you use your time will contribute to your mental health, physical health, wealth and overall wellbeing. Based on the average human lifespan, we are only living on Earth for typically less than eighty years.[149] That is less than eight decades and that is not even guaranteed! Use your time to better yourself now, so that you can enjoy your life in the near future.

You never know when it will be your time to die, so make the best of your life before your time is up. Many people further their education and master a profession. This can be very beneficial in making more money so that you can live a more enjoyable and stress-free life, since money is often a root cause of many stresses in life. Most people will spend the majority of their lives working. Thus, it is important to find a profession that you enjoy, while still making enough money to live comfortably and support your family.

Spend your time working and making money when you can, and save your money to invest in your future. For example, when you are young, try to work and save your money instead of going out clubbing every week. When you save enough, you can buy a property and rent it out to generate income, which can supplement your regular income from your job. Owning property can give you peace of mind knowing that you can potentially have rental income, as well as a property asset which is likely to appreciate over time. In the near future, over half of current jobs may be obsolete due to artificial intelligence, machines and automation.[150] Millions of people may become unemployed, and crime rates will increase as people will become desperate. It is far better to prepare for the future and be self-sufficient when times are good, rather than wait until it is too late and many job opportunities are lost.

Use your time to keep healthy and do not skip out on sleep. Sleep is of utmost importance and reduces stress, while repairing physical damage to your body and mind.[151] Sleep aids memory, helps prevent disease and builds new neuronal connections in the brain. Sleep on a comfortable mattress in a dark and quiet place.

Consider blackout curtains for your windows that can help eliminate outside light from entering your bedroom. If you have trouble sleeping, you can try breathing techniques that mimic your natural breathing patterns while you sleep. You can do this by taking short breaths in, and long breaths out.

Avoid consuming artificial sweeteners, chemicals, processed junk and fried foods that mess with your body's natural state of being and cause you to feel sluggish and unmotivated.[152] Allow the cells in your body to work well, utilizing a good diet which contributes to making you feel energized to do things in your life. Exercise regularly, as this burns off excess toxins[153] and releases mood boosting endorphins.[154] These recommendations sound fairly basic, but unfortunately, they have become a luxury in our modern fast-paced lives. These basic human needs are extremely important to maintaining good physical and mental wellbeing. You are only given one body in life. Treat it properly now, rather than taking expensive drugs with side effects later in life.[155]

Spending time doing an enjoyable activity with friends or a loved one can also heal you, and prevent you from focusing on past traumas. Interacting with people in a loving and caring environment where you are appreciated and safe, can make you feel as though the trauma you went through was not as severe. Isolation on the other hand, causes you to focus on the trauma and not move forward in life. It has become increasingly difficult to meet genuinely good people in the world. Though, if you can find one person or a small group of good people, then you should cherish them and spend time together to put your mind at ease. If you cannot find such genuine people in your life, then it may be best to live alone in peace. Do not settle or force disingenuous friendships with people who will use you or take advantage of you. This will cause you more pain and suffering.

Physical touch, cuddling and sex with a significant other, can also provide substantial healing capabilities for a person recovering from trauma or depression.[156] The romantic bond created between two people during an intimate session can stimulate sensations and hormones, which can relieve mental and physical stress and anxiety. I am not saying to go sleep around as this can cause more stress and sexually transmitted diseases. But consider having a romantic partner long-term, such as a caring spouse who can provide you with this comfort and stress relief. Likewise, ensure that you are equally positive and beneficial to them in similar or alternative ways.

Love yourself, love your life and love the environment that you live in. If there are aspects of your life that you hate, explore ways you can change them. For example, if you are working in telemarketing, getting yelled at daily while making minimum wage, it may be time to look into other morally sound professions which can pay more. High stress jobs do not always equal high pay. Strive to attain a stable job that would be more beneficial for your mental health. Though you may spend much of your life working, it is realistically acceptable to compromise, by having a career which you do not love, but also do not hate; provided your salary enables you to live your desired lifestyle. Sometimes, following your passion may not be financially beneficial. Do your research before you pursue a chosen career path in your life. If you can turn your passion into a profitable career that you love doing, this is a bonus in life.

Some consider their work as a form of peace in their daily routine. Whether it be an outlet to avoid an angry spouse, or a way to demonstrate their talents while performing their work duty as a form of art. There is a broad spectrum of professions, some which consist of high stress environments, and others which offer healing capabilities. Working in a job you are passionate about may not feel like work at all. Be it a factory, making cakes, wedding planning or photography, find your niche skill and run with it. Do not feel complacently trapped for the rest of your working life in your current monotonous job that you dislike. Likewise with jobs and with social friendship groups, if you feel unappreciated or unwanted, just leave. Make new friends, get a new job, move on and prosper.

Have a bed, a pillow, a car, and a home that you love. If you have financial constraints, you may not be able to live in your dream home at the current moment. In which case, appreciate what you have, as it may be far better than what many others have in the world. Many are homeless and do not know where or when they will have their next meal. You may be in a relationship, single or have an animal companion. Regardless of what you have in your current life, appreciate and cherish the positive in it. Even if you just have a bicycle, still take care of it and appreciate the good it does for you in your life. When you love and appreciate the things you currently have in your life, you will feel more content, peaceful, and happy with your overall life. A simple life is a peaceful one, having less complications to worry about. Appreciate the few good people you have in your life too, but do not be too vulnerable with your private information around them. Protect yourself.

For a few unfortunate souls, you may have been ruthlessly wronged by many people your entire life and need a fresh start to escape the stress before it kills you. In this case, look into moving out of the country or to a different state for a more peaceful life. Before you just skip this point thinking this is not a viable option, ask yourself why not? What is compelling you to be stuck in your current life dealing with stress? Your job you hate, that does not pay you enough? Your family that treats you like shit? Severe circumstances call for innovative thinking, and moving to a different country for better health may be one of the best decisions you ever make. Several countries, such as Costa Rica and parts of Europe, offer a good climate with many English-speaking natives. A cheaper cost of living and kinder people are added benefits.

Not everyone is cut out to be a lawyer, doctor or engineer. Some were screwed over by family, business partners and so-called "friends." Not everyone had equal opportunities in life to succeed in big cities with increasing housing and rental prices. You may feel trapped in your current situation, with bills accumulating which your salary cannot provide enough money to pay for. Before going deeper into debt, do research and travel to potential moving destinations. Indulge in the tasty local cuisine while you explore which place would best suit your life requirements. Learn a few native words to impress the locals. Many are very welcoming and happy to meet someone from a country that they admire.

There is no perfect place in the world, not America, not England and not Dubai. Every place has its benefits, as well as areas for improvement. You first need to evaluate your values, goals and the lifestyle you wish to realistically achieve. Once you figure out what matters to you and the desired lifestyle that you can afford, you can begin to research which countries you qualify to move to. Be realistic about your goals to avoid disappointment. Country laws and values can also differ drastically for matters such as LGBTQ people, marijuana, and the severity in punishment for crimes such as theft.[157] Some countries openly promote certain values, while others impose the death penalty for them.[158] Find a place in which your values best align with the country's objectives. This will help you better integrate and appreciate the country you call your new home.

Do not tell your enemies of your plans to relocate, as they may try something unimaginably evil to prevent you from achieving your happiness. Consider that you will likely forego many conveniences you have become accustomed to, such as high-speed internet, clean running tap water and stable electricity. You must also be aware of the differences in healthcare, petty crime, and locals charging you more for things because you are a foreigner. Moving countries is a big decision. Though, based on how severe the stress levels are for you in your current place of residence, moving may be a lifesaving measure preventing you from suicide or going mentally insane.

If you choose to seek professionally prescribed medical drugs to cope with your depression, trauma or anxiety, ensure that you are aware of the potential negative side effects to avoid additional strain in your life.[159] Many people may lack the life experience to fully comprehend the extent of the trauma you went through in life. They may not understand the emotions you feel and why you feel the way you do. They may have been raised in a developed Western country,[160] while your drunk father beat the shit out of you and starved you in the ghetto projects that you grew up in.[161] Talking to someone wanting to help you cope with your trauma or depression, will likely not assist you to recover your money that was stolen from you nor bring your dead child back to life. Some people may claim to have experienced similar traumatic events in their lives. However, many are unaware of exceptional cases deviating from the norm in society, and their experience may not be relevant to your specific trauma. For example, they may be older and unaware of modern, unique, and unprecedented situations which arise in modern society, as a by-product of technologies that did not exist when they were growing up.

Depending on the severity of the trauma caused to you by other people, you may wish to bring harm to the people who harmed you. However, if you were to be honest and say this, a professional may notify the authorities, and you will likely face some very uncomfortable questions.[162] This will further contribute to your trauma and stress. Realize that everyone in life faces different challenges and hardships. Yours may have been more severe than most. However, that does not give you the right to physically harm or kill another human life.

Some people are psychotic, selfish, violent beings without any conscience as to whom they hurt. They may seem pure evil to you based on their extremely harmful actions done towards you, which has negatively affected your life. But know that people are not perfect, people make mistakes, and that same person may change into someone good one day. Never use your anger to harm another person who harmed you. Instead, use your anger to push you forward in life to accomplish great things and forget about the trauma you went through. Dwelling on a past traumatic event prevents you from accomplishing great things and moving forward. Your time on Earth is short, so make the most of it for yourself. Often those who wronged you will end up facing their own traumatic issues without you having to do anything.

Knowledge and experience are important for understanding life and people. Consider how things work and came to be. Who wrote the first textbook on a subject before any textbooks existed on that topic? How did they gain their knowledge? Textbooks become updated and change with new discoveries, which disprove previous theories that were once regarded as factual. A layman may be ridiculed for their observations and theories on a matter, only to be proven correct years later. Decades ago, car engineers made cars very strong, thinking it would be safer in a crash. Later, it was discovered that this would cause the passengers to absorb the impact of the crash, instead of having crumple zones which could absorb the energy from the crash.[163] For a few, this may seem to be common sense while pondering things in their mind. Yet, when these few that think differently bring forth their ideas, they are often shunned, being told that they do not know what they are speaking of because they are not experts on the matter. Many will oppose your thoughts and suggestions in life. Do not argue with idiots. Often, no one will know what you observe in life, what you are going through, and what you may need in your life to be complete and happy.

When possible, isolate the cause of your stress and work towards avoiding it. Alternatively, try to improve your living situation so that the stress does not continue to have detrimental effects on your future life. We have but one life to live, and it is often much more peaceful to let the small things go. Forgiveness is key. If you wish to sleep well at night, practice forgiving others before you go to bed. Holding a grudge is like a punishment to yourself without the person who hurt you ever knowing how you feel. The wrongdoer will continue to live their life happily, while you get grey hair letting them live rent-free in your head. Dwelling on past traumatic events may potentially harm your health and cause you to go mentally insane, while the perpetrator feels nothing. Remember, life is not fair. If you cannot win, cannot change it, cannot remedy it or make them compensate you for your losses incurred using legal means, then let it go and move forward in your life.

A good approach in life is to understand the mentality of humans as a species. Forget about what the media tries to tell you, and what you were indoctrinated by society to believe. Laws are not always morally perfect. Innocent people have been sent to jail, then decades later proven innocent after society robbed them of their lives and tore their families away from them.[164] Being politically correct and pretending that we live in perfect harmony only masks the moral problems within the fabric of society. It conceals what is hidden deep within the thoughts of people. This can be dangerous if these people get the opportunity to release their inner most desires and enact their evil thoughts, such as in certain positions of power. Some remain silent, stay politically correct, and are too scared to voice their thoughts for fear of being called out on their racist beliefs. Many are prejudice, but will only reveal how they feel about a certain culture, religion, or group of people when they are around close friends or relatives who share similar views.[165]

Never feel envious of what others have; you are wasting time and energy needed to focus on achieving what you want in life. If you have no goals, then set some that you want to accomplish, and focus on them rather than thinking of past negative events. If you decide to turn to faith or religion, this can be therapeutic and a source of peace. You may ponder, how do humans and animals dream and have consciousness, which cannot be recreated in a laboratory. Artificial intelligence cannot compute the same judgement, creativity, natural emotions and thought processes that a human being can, without learning from past events. Ponder how humans procreate and have a biological clock.

Some look into a certain religion, and after learning about it, are convinced that God will serve people whatever punishment or reward they have earned in life. Some turn to religion as a coping mechanism, after experiencing traumatic events in their lives and observing life, death and the world around them. Many religions emphasize concepts such as forgiveness, compassion, and peace, which can help you with overcoming past trauma. Some faiths teach people that this life is only a test; a short passing, where people's conduct will determine if they will be rewarded with heaven or hell. A strong belief in faith will allow a person to sleep better at night. They can sleep knowing that life is short, and those who wronged them in this life will pay for their bad deeds in the afterlife. People who believe in God can go about their day in a more peaceful manner, knowing that what is meant for them will be. Thus, if they cannot recover what was taken from them by other people in life, they will be compensated for it later. Belief in a religion can be nourishment for your soul, similar to how fruits and vegetables provide nourishment to your body.

We live on Earth a certain number of years and do things that affect the world and others around us. We may build roads, write books and teach others. Then we die and science cannot explain what happens to our minds or souls after death. Where do we go? For these reasons, many turn to belief in God. We have speech to communicate and understand each other. How does our mind work to understand other human beings conversing with us? How do we have nerves built-in to our body so that we can move and feel pain when we are injured? How can we feel temperature? We are miraculous forms of life on planet Earth. Perhaps there really is more to it. Regardless of whether you choose to believe in God or not, for your own health, you need to come to the realization that whatever incident happened in your past has already happened, and we cannot change that.

We cannot sue everyone for every little thing. We cannot spend countless hours chasing down people who may have hit our vehicles in the parking lot in the past. Even your own relatives and friends might continue to open your car door and bang it against a stranger's car parked beside yours. They do not care about your property nor the stranger's car, because it is not their own. We must sadly accept that some people will commit heinous, cruel, and unjust things to us, and they will not be punished in life. This is the reality we must face, accept, and move forward from. Otherwise, you will spend your entire life chasing after other people instead of living your own life. Come to the realization that this life we live is a temporary one. We will all die in due time, and we never know when that time may come, be it in young or old age.

This life is not fair. Repeat, this life is not fair. People will wrong you. People who you think are your friends will backstab you. Your best friend may sleep with your spouse or breakup your marriage. Your wife may run up the line of credit on your mortgage-free house and steal your money. For some unfortunate few of us, our own parents will take away our rights from us. Some parents can be unjustly violent towards their innocent child when the kid had not done any wrong. Some fathers rape their own daughters. Some parents sell their children for money or force their child to marry an abusive spouse whom they do not find any appeal in.[166] Your roommate may steal your rental deposit money and leave town. Again, I repeat, THIS LIFE IS NOT FAIR. The sooner you realize this key point, the sooner you may very likely be able to move forward with your current situation in life, knowing that your life will not be entirely perfect.

Do not overthink things as this will waste your time. You may sometimes even be worried of a thing that potentially may never come to be. Live in the present, using lessons from your past to protect yourself while preparing for your best future. You may be overly cautious, and afraid to take a risk on your business ideas because you are afraid of failing or concerned of what people might think. Have more self-confidence and work towards your goals with a balanced approach. It is good to be cautious, but do not be afraid of everything in life, such as applying to be a manager at work, or getting married to a person whom you have known for many years and talk about everything together. Take your precautions, have a backup plan, get things in writing, and take a few calculated risks which may or may not change your future.

Try to find one person you can trust in life. This is very difficult as most people are selfish. Though, perhaps there is someone you met in your childhood, at work, or a family member who cares about you but you never really considered to be very close to. If they share personal information about themselves with you, then this is a good indicator that they at least somewhat trust you. A noteworthy characteristic trait, would also be that they do not unjustly speak ill of others to you. Once you know their values, you may be able to gradually open up with things you may need an opinion on, such as taking an educational course or changing careers. In these mentoring friendship relationships, it is still important to guard yourself with things such as your financial status and your big goals or relationships, as you never know what a person is truly thinking. They are human, and may still feel envy and greed, which may overpower their willingness to help you. It is unfortunate that we may find it very difficult to trust another human after a very traumatic event in our life. But this is the reality for many, and our brains are wired to put up barrier walls to protect ourselves from being hurt again in future. Listen to your gut instinct.

When someone commits rape against you, kills someone you love, severely injures you, or steals a significant amount of money from you which negatively changes your life plans, you may think about it every day for the rest of your life. Some rape victims constantly relive the trauma within their minds, making it difficult for them to feel comfortable having an intimate partner and enjoy sex. Some try to block the event out of their memory and force themselves not to think about it, while avoiding situations that remind them of the incident.

Constantly replaying the traumatic event in one's mind can affect healthy sleep patterns and can cause the person to develop memory loss.[167] In severe instances, they may have symptoms of schizophrenia,[168] hear voices,[169] and have impaired judgment where their brain no longer allows them to think rationally for the consequences of their actions.[170] They may obsess over hurting the person who raped or otherwise harmed them. They may experience dreams of killing that person and wake up not knowing if they actually killed the person or not. In order to heal and overcome trauma caused to you by others, you must reshape your entire mindset on how you look at life.

If you do not get over your trauma, your mind will be preoccupied with living in your past. You might be doing something such as watching a hit new movie, but your mind will not register what your eyes are seeing. You will go through the movie and your life without living it, because you are consumed with your internal thoughts and feeling sorry for yourself, which ultimately leads to punishing yourself. As a result, you will not remember many things you do in life. You must learn to turn your mind away from constantly focussing on the ones who wronged you and traumatized your life. In your daily life activities, focus your mind, energy and body on what you are presently experiencing. Pay attention in class, enjoy social events and focus on your work.

Identify your trigger points that can suddenly make you tense and anxious. This could be thinking of a stressful past experience, being in a particular place, smelling a certain fragrance or listening to a specific song that reminds you of a traumatic event from your past. Try to avoid these triggers which cause your mind to constantly think of that incident. In addition, try to avoid conversational topics around the issue to help you move forward and not be reminded of it. If you must, move apartments and change your furniture for your mental wellbeing. This is to help you move on and focus on making the best future you can from your current situation. Dwelling on the past will hold you back further in life, so you need to change your mindset.

Do not take things too seriously in life when others wrong you. Realize that this life is not perfect, and this life is short. Try your best to make the most of it, and as hard as you try, things still may not go the way you want. Know that you tried your best, and know that some people are just selfish pricks. Although you feel your life would be better if a person did not do you wrong, you still have the rest of your life to live. Be grateful for the things you still have, hopefully including good health and some wealth left to build back a better future for yourself. Hopefully, the mentally deranged evil individuals will be punished in some other way, even if you cannot take them to court or have them justly taken care of in your life. They may already be punishing, and you just cannot see it because they are no longer a part of your life.

Do not cloud your mind with worries, regret, and depression. A clean mind can be more creative and have many fresh ideas to help you in life, potentially generating more income than what you may have lost. Thinking of things such as past rape or having a loved one murdered, may make it harder for you to feel love, and prevent you from meeting someone who can greatly fill your emptiness. This person could potentially bring you happiness that you cannot even imagine. You were wronged, you are the victim, and that sucks. However, do not let the evil person who damaged you continue to ruin your future life, by remaining stuck in your depressed mental state and making no effort to move forward.

It is okay to have your guard up and be very cautious to avoid being taken advantage of or abused again in future. Remove yourself from toxic relationships and block those people out of your life. Staying in a friendship or relationship in which you are taken advantage of, can cause you to develop health issues. After prolonged stress from dealing with people, you may begin to have shaky hands,[171] slurred speech,[172] and memory loss.[173] Therefore, it is best to leave those people behind. However, do not block out people who are genuinely good, as these people are rare to find.

If you are a soft-hearted individual, it is okay for you to want people to trust you first before you eventually trust them. You went through trauma, and now you must protect yourself from going through similar traumatic events in future. Many people will say that happiness is a state of mind and that you can simply wake up and choose to be happy. The people that say this may refuse to admit that they also get stressed and angry in life. They may even have difficulty controlling their anger at times and become very aggressive towards another person during a dispute. These people often have never been severely tortured or traumatized by others.

They never had to deal with extreme forms of violence, sexual abuse, or other oppressive actions from people.

To heal ourselves from past trauma and stresses so that we can progress in life, we must drastically change the way we look at life entirely. Consider this, we are merely a glimpse in the timeline of the planet we live on, and we have evidence proving that great civilizations and dinosaurs have walked the Earth and crumbled before us.[174] Contemplate the universe, the billions of stars, and galaxies with hidden planets still undiscovered.[175] We are just a minuscule speck in the universe, on a planet so perfectly distanced from the Sun that it can sustain life. Our lives are short, and many significant things we experience daily, science will still fail to accurately explain before we die.[176] The next time someone wrongs us, ponder if it is worth the time in our lives to take action against them, or if you wish to let the power in the universe handle them and serve justice.

An important strategy to heal yourself from past trauma and look at life positively again, would be to find your exit in life. Find your passion in life that makes you enthusiastically thrilled. Your passion can be a sport you love to play, documentaries, motorcycles, computer coding or a hobby that fascinates you. Some people also find comfort in a valued object they possess such as a teddy bear, handbag, watch, their car or even a smartphone. When you begin to remember your tragic life events that make you depressed, train yourself to stop thinking about them immediately and focus on your passion. Have fun in life and indulge yourself in your passion within moderation. If for example, you love bicycles and riding, treat yourself to that expensive bicycle that costs a few thousand dollars if you can afford it. Do not listen to others who tell you that the price tag is ridiculous. Your mental and physical health are more important long-term. It is not their passion, so they will not understand the value of a carbon fiber frame and ceramic brakes.[177]

Do things that make you happy in life. You may be saving your favourite shoes, dress or perfume for a special occasion. However, you do not know when your last day alive on Earth will be. Enjoy the possessions you worked hard to earn while you can still enjoy them. Why save things until they expire, no longer fit you, or get damaged or taken away from you? When you are young, and especially if you are trying to attract a romantic partner, dress good, smell good and get a nice haircut. Drive your nice car or ride your Ducati motorcycle to the office just because you feel like it. Some things such as joy and happiness cannot be calculated in a specific unit of measurement. If it makes you happy, it can help release feel-good hormones in your body, which can help heal you.

Avoid excessively stressing over things such as money. You may be saving for that special purchase or marriage, then die before you get to enjoy it. In the end, your family that screwed you over may get to enjoy your wealth while they laugh at your pitiful life. Try your best in life, work hard and save your money, but treat yourself moderately along your journey. Do not take things for granted. Be grateful for your blessings in life. You may have a life that you hate, which many in this world dream of living. Do not have too much self-pity in life and be careful not to complain to others who do not care about your problems. Many will only be happy to hear of your misfortune and give you bad advice regarding your loss.

Know what you want in life, protect yourself, and keep your goals private while you work hard towards achieving them.

In first world countries, people often work very hard until they die. They need a vacation to escape the stress and take their minds away from tight deadlines and staring at a computer screen. In third world countries, people want a vacation to break away from the mundane simple life that they live. If you come from a fast-paced working environment, you might find relief in a slower-paced region, such as in the Caribbean or Latin America. Whereas, if you live an already slow-paced lifestyle such as in a village, then you may crave to escape to a busy city for a holiday to see tall buildings and people rushing to their meetings during the day. The grass always seems greener on the other side, and many people will sacrifice their time, health, and happiness to live in big cities and drive luxury cars. Many of these people get old and wish they had retired earlier to move back to their home country in the village that their parents raised them in.

Regardless of your situation, if you are trying your best in life, then do not stress the rest. Know that you gave it your all, and whatever else you wanted but could not achieve was not meant for you. Everything happens for a reason. We are all connected, and there are things in this world which science cannot explain. We can plan our best and things may not go our way. Yet other times, miracles can happen that change our lives around unexpectedly in a positive manner. Have faith and do your best in life, while not harming innocent people along your journey. Otherwise, you can cause them undue stress and pain which they can hold a grudge over.

Do not blindly listen to the advice of others in life. Most people are too proud to admit when they are wrong or do not know the answer to something. They might feed you incorrect and potentially damaging information. It is better to do your own research and trust yourself in life. Strive to be independent so you do not need to depend on others in life. Learn to never depend on others for your happiness. When people earn your trust and run away with your life savings or cheat on you, it will cause you unexpected pain inside. You may feel anxiety, depression, anger and hopelessness, which can negatively affect your physical health. Follow your own passions and goals to create your own mental peace and happiness in your life.

It is okay to block some people out for a short while to accomplish your goals, but respect those who were good to you. Keep good company so that you can mentally live a peaceful, happy life, and fulfill your highest potential in growth. If you have a trustworthy romantic partner, talk with them in private about difficulties you face in life without telling outsiders. Often, a second opinion on a matter from a trustworthy individual, such as your spouse, can help you overcome a problem with ease. However, the advice from some family and friends may lead you down the wrong path, even when they are genuinely trying to help. Especially avoid taking advice from biased family and friends relating to your marriage, relationship or situationship.

Studies show that many farmers live happy and fulfilled lives while exposing themselves to nature. Try to immerse yourself in activities that expose you to nature regularly. Consider gardening if you have the space, even if it is a small garden on your balcony or by your window. The act of caring for another living organism, even if it is a plant, can help give you purpose in life. Similarly, spending quality time with animals has been proven as therapeutic and assists with improving mental wellbeing.[178] This is especially true if you do not have any humans to show you mutual love in life. Live a healthy and fulfilled life.

You may feel as though throughout your entire life you have always been nice to others, giving and helping those who ask for favours. Yet, they only take, and continually demand more from you without reciprocating equal kindness in your friendship. You feel used, taken advantage of and strained for time. Stop now and start doing things for yourself that bring you joy. There are only twenty-four hours in a day, and a third of that should be used for sleep. After a working shift, travel time and eating, you may be left with only four hours in a day to use with your discretion.

There is no such thing as "making time to do things." You either have the time or you end up cutting into your sleep. Be realistic and use your time wisely for your own mental health. Do not continue being nice to others while causing stress to yourself in the process. Use your time for your own needs and wants, then with any remaining time you have, you may assist those in need. This can contribute to improving your contentment with yourself, and make you feel more satisfied with the life you live.

Purchase a pair of comfortable shoes that support your entire body weight and grip the ground beneath you. As well, invest in items that make your life more convenient and less stressful. A phone that works well, a warm winter coat in a cold climate, and tools you need to make money. If you are constantly lifting heavy groceries from the car to your condo apartment, consider buying a small trolley cart which relieves pressure from your back and knees. Do not waste money spending lavishly, but invest in things related to protecting your health. You may start enjoying things you once found stressful, such as ice-skating in the freezing cold, while using your new winter coat and gloves.

Practice natural habits such as grounding, where you walk barefoot on the grass to benefit from your body electrically grounding itself with the Earth.[179] It is unfortunate that many of us live busy lives, in big cities surrounded by pollution, and deal with aggressive angry people daily. Your schedule may be very hectic, so your home should be a sanctuary where you can relieve your stress. Not everyone can afford to travel for a holiday annually. Having a comfortable home can reduce your stress levels and make you satisfied with not being able to get away often. You can decorate with plants, new curtains and an ergonomic sofa that you find comfort in. Make your home reflect your style and suit your needs. You can even save a space for prayer if you have the square footage available.

Regardless of if you are an atheist, spiritual, or someone who believes solely in science; the universe, life, and nature, are things which we cannot deny. If we go to bed with malice in our hearts every night, this can contribute to causing actual damage to our hearts. Many people who suffer heart attacks in their twenties and thirties, have been through stress or trauma, which has caused their physical and mental health to deteriorate.[180] Do not overwork yourself excessively, or you may not get to enjoy what you worked so hard for. Life may pass you by as you miss seeing your kids grow up. You may even miss out on having kids altogether if you continue overworking yourself. Go to bed with a clean heart and ponder how the universe is so big, and we are so small. Our souls are in our bodies that miraculously can heal themselves, reproduce and create life. Do not overthink nor worry about those who have wronged us. One day their fun may come to an end, and they may get cancer. Live your life, and focus on your future.

Many people in life have loved ones to turn to for comfort and support when recovering from a traumatic experience. Family, friends, loved ones or especially a romantic significant other, would be a great help. Find someone to turn to who genuinely cares for your wellbeing without being paid to listen to you. Find someone who is willing to take the time to listen to you and understand your situation, such as dealing with a unique modern societal problem in woke times. In modern times, people are more connected by the internet, yet far more disconnected with in-person conversations than with generations before smartphones. Sometimes when facing traumatic occurrences, we just need a hug to uplift our mood. Though for some, no amount of talking to people will help overcome the effects of the traumatic experience. If they do not help themselves by changing their mindset, these victims will live and dwell on their trauma for the rest of their lives.

Unfortunately, some of us may live lonely lives, with no parents, nor siblings, nor romantic partners to turn to for support. If you do not have anyone to turn to in your current situation, do not seek help from someone who will take advantage of your desperate need for attention. They will use you, which will cause you to regret ever knowing them. Instead, realize that this is your situation now, and assess the damage done. Block the trauma out so that you are not constantly thinking of it. Then, try your utmost best to make a recovery plan, and follow through with it to rebuild your life.

When you are making friends in life, do not be too reliant on them. They may have families who love, care and back them up, which you may lack. So do not look to fill a void in your life with friends who you think you can trust, but in reality, they do not look at you the same way. They might be using your friends' circle only to have a good time. They will likely cut you out the moment you are no longer convenient or a contributing asset. Treat your friends as people you can socialize and connect with while playing sports and eating out together. But do not expect your friendships to last a lifetime, as it may or may not happen.

A friend does not owe you anything for being your friend. They can move away to another country, without any consideration of your friendship in their decision-making process. You are a tool, something that provides them with support and laughter. You are not necessarily more valuable than their family, careers or romantic interests. Your friend could fall in love with another friend of yours. Even though they met through you, they might both decide to cut you out of their lives. Understand this and treat your "friends" accordingly. Likewise, as you go through life and make new connections, do not harm innocent people. Treat others with respect until they begin to impose on your own rights. Then you can become assertive and stand up for yourself from the start of the abuse. Seek outside help from others if necessary.

Do not slander another person's name solely because you have a disagreement with them or their views. If they did not take your property and did not physically or otherwise harm you, then respect their right to their own beliefs and opinions and let them be. You have not lost anything from them, even if you strongly feel that their beliefs are incorrect.

Also, do not be put down by liars slandering your name, or people speaking aggressively and condescendingly towards you. Try your best to calmly stand up for yourself and advise people that you did not do what they say you did. Understand that they are wrong, they are liars, and likely they might just be jealous of you, so insulting you with their lies is all that they can do. You can simply pull out your phone, record them where legally possible, and if you wish, take legal action against them.

When you are dealing with people such as in traffic, and someone becomes verbally irate while speaking to you, make the choice to ignore them and drive away to avoid dealing with them or escalating the situation. Do not get upset easily over small matters that do not affect you long-term. How can you let an idiot ruin your entire day? If you were wrong though, apologize, improve yourself, and move on. Focus on important things in your life, such as your job, family, place you wish to move to next, or other goals you have. Block people out of your life who bring you down, you do not owe each other anything.

It is unfortunate when people take from us without having the right to, but we must overcome. Many before us have been raped in history, had their land and property stolen and had their loved ones killed. Unfortunately, this is life. Trials we face as humans, caused by other humans. Try your best to make the most of it and move on. You will not always get full compensation; the same way your car insurance company will only give you a depreciated amount for your once brand-new car if it is stolen. But be strong and move forward to improve your current situation in life. Do not waste your limited time and energy dwelling on an unchangeable situation. Plan something new and bigger, and daydream about it regularly as motivation towards accomplishing it in life.

Chapter 8: Island Theory

So how can you protect yourself from modern society stress and the rising cost of living? It has reached a breaking point for many, where people are choosing between paying rent or buying groceries.[181] There was a brilliant engineer in the 1960's, by the name of Giorgio Rosa. He constructed a platform situated on international waters off the coast of Italy. This engineer declared himself the president of his man-made "island," and declared its independence on June 24th, 1968. It was a short-lived dream, and showed the world what one man can do to free himself and others from the restraints of modern government.[182]

There are several islands in the world for sale that cost less than a 2-bedroom apartment in New York City. I have a concept to start an island nation inhabited by a small population. Depending on the size of the island, the population may be approximately ten to one hundred people initially, each contributing a specialized skill to this newfound society. A Doctor, engineer, carpenter, farmer, welder and fisherman as examples. These individuals would possess the necessary skills and knowledge to survive and establish a community on the said island. This island would be self-sufficient, sustaining our own vegetation and livestock. No motorized vehicles would be present, and each family would be gifted two horses to use as they wish. We would harness the power of the wind and the ocean waves to generate electricity, and the majority of waste would be biodegradable or recyclable. There would be an education system established and a medical center as well. However, do not expect to find a place to buy plastic battery operated toys or designer clothes. You make what you wear or have the nation's seamstress sew it for you. Kids will be taught essential duties, and education will start at an early age.

After a monetary currency is established, no loans or interest would be permitted, as interest creates inflation.[183] The goal of the island would be to establish a long-term, self-sustaining community, independent from the rest of the world. We will not be affected by global recessions or stock market crashes. In theory, people will be happy, as they will not be judged by the clothes they wear or the car they drive. People will not struggle to pay monthly installments on their houses since they would not be tied to a mortgage. Hard work will be rewarded, and if you want something, you must work and save until you can afford to buy it full in cash. Conversely, with most economies around the world today, if the builder can build fifty homes a year, and one hundred people are able to apply for a loan, an increased demand would be created for the limited supply of homes available. This in turn causes inflation of home prices for future generations.

Essentially, my island nation would aim to eliminate inflation, which most interest-based first world economies are suffering from. There should not be economic cycles, recessions, varying interest rates which affect people's mortgages, and inflation caused by increasing minimum wage among other factors.[184] On my island nation, these vicious economic cycles, along with many other stresses people face in most countries, will essentially be eliminated. No one living outside of the island will be allowed to purchase a home nor any land on the island. This may sound selfish, but I have to take care of my citizens. Of course, this is a theoretical exercise, and the practical application of my theories are yet to be proven.

In the meanwhile, you can still take steps to protect yourself from ever increasing living costs, and laws which limit your ability to live freely in a way which you strive for. If you are stuck living in the city due to your job or caring for a loved one, you can consider establishing a small vegetable garden, and growing your own organic food. This will save costs from the grocery store and ensure you are taking a step towards self-dependency. Learn new skills, such as vehicle maintenance, fishing, cooking and survival in the wild for unexpected circumstances.

You do not necessarily need an island to escape your current depressive life. Love the place you live in. You may relocate to find happiness in a smaller town within your country. Some countries such as Canada, offer a variety of different vibes in different provinces. Consider a slower paced lifestyle in Prince Edward Island, Newfoundland or Alberta as examples. We are all humans, passing through life which we have but a short time to enjoy. Comprehend that we will face trauma in life, and it is important to grasp the big picture. Do not let those few traumatic experiences ruin your entire life. Do not shape your future based on your abusive past. Learn from the past. Examine your present situation. Then set a new target and focus on achieving it, so that you can enjoy what is left of your precious life on planet Earth.

About the Author

Tariq Ahad is a Canadian-born writer, with his ground-breaking first book titled "How to Deal with Trauma from People and Thrive in Woke Times." Mr. Ahad comes from a lower middle-class family in Toronto, Canada, and has experience teaching youth within the community. In his free time, he enjoys riding motorcycles, working with animals and serving humanity through various charity efforts in the Greater Toronto Area.

References

Disclaimer: As a teenager and in my early twenties, I was inclined to watch documentaries and listen to the news for comfort and entertainment. I have never been to a concert, never been drunk and never smoked a cigarette in my life. I strived to seek knowledge and educate myself on facts and events within the world. I wrote this book from my head entirely, based on news articles I remember from decades ago, and events and facts I recall through my life thus far. I also utilized much of my personal life experiences, such as self-observations made while suffering stress and trauma myself. When I mention points such as severe trauma causing people to potentially hear voices, it is because I have experienced this myself. As an underweight teenager, I worked in a warehouse where I sustained back spinal issues from repeatedly lifting heavy boxes. Later in my life I worked in an office for a large corporation. In this office I had an ergonomic assessment completed that concluded I was in need of an ergonomic chair. After years of waiting, I finally had a worker deliver an ergonomic chair which perfectly suited my needs. I signed off on this chair and took my lunch break. While away from my desk, the delivery worker sneakily swapped the chair I signed off on, for a subpar chair which was extremely uncomfortable for me. When I returned from my lunch break and noticed the original chair was no longer at my workstation, I spoke with my colleague who witnessed the switch and I immediately contacted the professional department in charge. I was advised the delivery worker stated he called me and confirmed I gave him approval to switch the chair. This call never took place. The experts then proceeded to claim that the new subpar unergonomic chair was in fact the correct chair for me. My co-worker can confirm this entire story. During another stage in my life, I visited a well-known dental office where the dental assistant cleaned my teeth and advised me that I have no cavities. The owner of the establishment came into the office and said, "We'll see about that," and claimed that I have a large cavity that required urgent filling, though I felt no pain at all. He drilled my teeth and hit a nerve, then filled it and charged my insurance company accordingly. For several months the pain was so intense that I could not even eat soft rice using that tooth. His solution was installing a crown, which I declined. If I were to state certain facts in this book based on my life experiences without any scientific basis, many would proclaim that I am making things up. Therefore, the following references can be used to assist and relate to the facts and statistics written in this book. These references may or may not directly relate to the information written in this book.

1. Lee, S. (n.d.). *Does stress cause cancer?* Canadian Cancer Society. https://cancer.ca/en/cancer-information/reduce-your-risk/myths-and-controversies/does-stress-cause-cancer#:~:text=A%20weakened%20immune%20system%20plays,greater%20risk%20of%20developing%20cancer.
2. New Radicals band. (1998). *You Get What You Give.*
3. Harvard Health. (2014, March 9). *In brief: Hugs heartfelt in more ways than one.* https://www.health.harvard.edu/newsletter_article/In_brief_Hugs_heartfelt_in_more_ways_than_one
4. Renoe, E. (2018b, May 21). *Are men starving for physical touch?* Ethan Renoe. https://ethanrenoe.com/2017/04/04/are-men-starving-for-physical-touch/
5. Tunney, C. (2018, January 31). Trudeau says zero tolerance on misconduct toward women applies to him as well. *CBC.* https://www.cbc.ca/news/politics/trudeau-careful-metoo-1.4511093
6. Wisevoter. (2023, May 3). *Rape Statistics by Country 2023 - Wisevoter.* https://wisevoter.com/country-rankings/rape-statistics-by-country/
7. *Auto theft.* (n.d.). https://data.torontopolice.on.ca/pages/auto-theft
8. National Post Staff. (2013, March 12). "Lucky Moose Bill" loosens self-defence, citizen's arrest laws. *Nationalpost.* https://nationalpost.com/news/toronto/lucky-moose-bill-loosens-self-defence-citizens-arrest-laws
9. Tiwari, A. (2023, July 21). Women's Safety Crisis: Rise in sexual harassment, assault complaints in India. *India Today.* https://www.indiatoday.in/diu/story/womens-safety-crisis-rise-in-sexual-harassment-assault-complaints-india-2410074-2023-07-21
10. PharmD, J. C. (2023, March 20). *Side effects of Prozac: What you need to know.* Healthline. https://www.healthline.com/health/drugs/prozac-side-effects
11. Freshwater, P. (2023, February 26). *People who have been declared clinically dead explain what happens when you die.* The Mirror. https://www.mirror.co.uk/news/us-news/people-who-been-declared-clinically-29294562
12. Browne, A. (2017, December 2). Dentists ruin teeth for profit. *The Guardian.* https://www.theguardian.com/society/2000/apr/16/futureofthenhs.health
13. Diwakar, A. (2022, June 8). US accounted for 73 percent of global mass shootings. *US Accounted for 73 Percent of Global Mass Shootings.* https://www.trtworld.com/magazine/us-accounted-for-73-percent-of-global-mass-shootings-12787908
14. Balakrishnan, A. (2010). The Development of Moral Education in Malaysia. *Asia Pacific Journal of Educators and Education, Vol.25. 89-101.*

http://web.usm.my/apjee/APJEE_25_2010/APJEE_25_06_Vishalache%20(89-101).pdf

15. Appleton, R. (2021, December 22). Holiday shopping brawls: How Tickle Me Elmo, Nintendo 64 taught us the meaning of Christmas. *Indianapolis Star*. https://www.indystar.com/story/news/2021/12/22/christmas-gifts-holiday-shopping-tickle-me-elmo-nintendo-64-caused-brawls-25-years-ago/8924612002/

16. *On gun violence, the United States is an outlier*. (n.d.). The Institute for Health Metrics and Evaluation. https://www.healthdata.org/news-events/insights-blog/acting-data/gun-violence-united-states-outlier

17. Lewis, T. (2023, April 6). YouTube creator shot while filming prank in mall food court. *FOX 5 DC*. https://www.fox5dc.com/news/youtube-prank-could-be-cause-of-dulles-town-center-shooting

18. Sky News. (2023, May 11). Who is Josef Fritzl? The rapist who kept his daughter locked in a cellar for 24 years. *Sky News*. https://news.sky.com/story/who-is-josef-fritzl-the-rapist-who-kept-his-daughter-locked-in-a-cellar-for-24-years-12878269

19. G S C Benson. (1975). *Causes and Cures of Political corruption | Office of Justice Programs*. https://www.ojp.gov/ncjrs/virtual-library/abstracts/causes-and-cures-political-corruption

20. McRae, D. (2023, March 26). *Church closures and the loss of community social Capital | PANL Prospects*. https://carleton.ca/panl/2023/church-closures-and-the-loss-of-community-social-capital-by-don-mcrae/

21. Chaya, L. (2023, February 21). Ontario man charged with second-degree murder after alleged shooting of home invader. *Nationalpost*. https://nationalpost.com/news/milton-man-charged-second-degree-murder-home-invasion

22. MSEd, K. C. (2022, November 7). *What is the Fight-or-Flight response?* Verywell Mind. https://www.verywellmind.com/what-is-the-fight-or-flight-response-2795194

23. A GTA man took just an hour to find his dad's stolen car. But police say it wasn't a great idea. (2023, February 4). *CBC*. https://www.cbc.ca/news/canada/toronto/car-theft-rise-halton-region-oakville-place-1.6736013

24. Cineas, F. (2023, October 17). Palestine and BLM: The long history of Black solidarity with Palestinians and Jews. *Vox*. https://www.vox.com/2023/10/17/23918689/black-palestinian-solidarity-jewish-alliance-israel

25. U.S. Slavery: Timeline, Figures & Abolition. (2009, November 12). *HISTORY*. https://www.history.com/topics/black-history/slavery

26. Fixico, D. L. (2023, July 11). *When Native Americans were slaughtered in the name of 'Civilization.'* HISTORY. https://www.history.com/news/native-americans-genocide-united-states

27. Adam, J. (2023, March 20). When Could Women Open A Bank Account? *Forbes Advisor.* https://www.forbes.com/advisor/banking/when-could-women-open-a-bank-account/#:~:text=It%20wasn%27t%20until%201974,a%20signature%20from%20their%20husbands.

28. Powell, L. (2012, May 3). *NC court gives thumbs down to 'rule of thumb' – NC Miscellany.* https://blogs.lib.unc.edu/ncm/2012/05/03/nc-court-gives-thumbs-down-to-rule-of-thumb/

29. Egede, L. E., Walker, R. J., Campbell, J. A., Linde, S., Hawks, L., & Burgess, K. M. (2023). Modern Day Consequences of historic redlining: Finding a path forward. *Journal of General Internal Medicine, 38*(6), 1534–1537. https://doi.org/10.1007/s11606-023-08051-4

30. *Israel's settlements have no legal validity, constitute flagrant violation of international law, Security Council reaffirms | UN Press.* (2016, December 23). https://press.un.org/en/2016/sc12657.doc.htm

31. McCarthy, J. (2020, December 4). PHOTOS: Why these World War II sex slaves are still demanding justice. *NPR.* https://www.npr.org/sections/goatsandsoda/2020/12/04/940819094/photos-there-still-is-no-comfort-for-the-comfort-women-of-the-philippines

32. *The Perilous Fight . Financing the War | PBS.* (n.d.). https://www.pbs.org/perilousfight/home_front/financing_the_war/

33. Fontinelle, A. (2023, August 28). *A brief history of taxes in the U.S.* Investopedia. https://www.investopedia.com/articles/tax/10/history-taxes.asp

34. Paas-Lang, C. (2022, April 9). Canada pledges additional $100M in humanitarian aid to Ukraine. *CBC.* https://www.cbc.ca/news/politics/100-million-humanitarian-aid-harsh-rhetoric-1.6414657

35. EHealth scandal a $1B waste: auditor. (2009, October 8). *CBC.* https://www.cbc.ca/news/canada/toronto/ehealth-scandal-a-1b-waste-auditor-1.808640

36. Mothership., & Yeo, G. (2023, February 26). *US' dominance for past 40 years was 'never sustainable', but it will likely stay a key global power: S'pore's ex-foreign minister George Yeo.* Mothership.SG - News From Singapore, Asia and Around the World. https://mothership.sg/2023/02/us-dominance-george-yeo-musings/

37. Mallees, N. A., The Canadian Press. (2023, September 22). Canada to provide Ukraine with $650 million for armoured vehicles in new pledge of

support. *Nationalpost*. https://nationalpost.com/news/canada/what-canada-is-pledging-for-ukraine

38. National Post. (2023, September 29). Michel Maisonneuve: Cutting \$1B from our already underfunded military is preposterous. *Nationalpost*. https://nationalpost.com/opinion/cutting-1b-from-our-already-underfunded-military-is-simply-preposterous

39. National Post Staff. (2023, August 14). Ontario mayor who lives with her parents says she can't afford to buy a home in her municipality. *Nationalpost*. https://nationalpost.com/news/ontario-mayor-who-lives-with-her-parents-says-she-cant-afford-to-buy-a-home-in-her-municipality

40. O'Brien, A. (2021, December 9). A majority of Toronto's Generation Z have given up on the dream of owning a single-family home: report. *CTV News Toronto*. https://toronto.ctvnews.ca/a-majority-of-toronto-s-generation-z-have-given-up-on-the-dream-of-owning-a-single-family-home-report-1.5698817

41. Cohn, M. R. (2015, March 30). PC blunder over Highway 407 looms over Liberals on Hydro: Cohn. *Toronto Star*. https://www.thestar.com/politics/provincial/pc-blunder-over-highway-407-looms-over-liberals-on-hydro-cohn/article_ad35dd8f-bcfb-51a6-9bc6-a1b00fe0c5ef.html

42. S, Alicja. (2019, April 6). Worst deal ever? The 407 is worth \$30B today – Ontario sold it for 3.1B in 1999. Yahoo Finance. https://ca.finance.yahoo.com/news/worst-deal-ever-the-407-is-worth-30-b-today-ontario-sold-it-for-31-b-in-1998-181642680.html

43. Crawley, M. (2017, December 9). How privatized power haunts Ontario politics. *CBC*. https://www.cbc.ca/news/canada/toronto/ontario-hydro-bills-privatization-1.4439500

44. Oprean, C. (2020, February 4). Vancouver & Toronto Among Top 10 Most Expensive Cities in the World. *Point2 News*. https://www.point2homes.com/news/canada-real-estate/vancouver-toronto-among-top-10-most-expensive-cities-in-the-world.html

45. Poshnjari, I. (2023, October 4). *Toronto housing construction is 10 years behind: TRREB analyst - BNN Bloomberg.* BNN. https://www.bnnbloomberg.ca/toronto-s-housing-construction-is-10-years-behind-trebb-analyst-says-1.1980162

46. DeMattia, N. (2023, May 4). Rivian R1T Fender Bender turns into \$42,000 repair bill. *The Drive*. https://www.thedrive.com/news/rivian-r1t-fender-bender-turns-into-42000-repair-bill

47. Brigham, K. (2023, July 7). Why the electric vehicle boom could put a major strain on the U.S. power grid. *CNBC*. https://www.cnbc.com/2023/07/01/why-the-ev-boom-could-put-a-major-strain-on-our-power-grid.html

48. Ritchie, H. (2023, July 28). Is cobalt the blood diamond of electric cars? What can be done about it? *Sustainability by numbers*. https://www.sustainabilitybynumbers.com/p/cobalt

49. Cao, S. (2023, March 30). Two-Thirds of jobs are at risk: Goldman Sachs A.I. study. *Observer*. https://observer.com/2023/03/generative-a-i-may-replace-300-million-jobs-goldman-sachs-study/

50. Cecco, L. (2022, May 11). Are Canadians being driven to assisted suicide by poverty or healthcare crisis? *The Guardian*. https://www.theguardian.com/world/2022/may/11/canada-cases-right-to-die-laws

51. *Home - CRWC*. (n.d.). https://www.wrongfulconvictions.ca/

52. Hernandez, M. (2023, October 3). Residents of LA's notorious Skid Row talk survival amid ODs, gangs and dead rats in the walls. *New York Post*. https://nypost.com/2023/10/03/residents-of-las-skid-row-talk-about-survival-in-the-impoverished-area/

53. O'Mary, L. (2023, August 11). Suicides in U.S. Reached All-Time High in 2022: CDC. *WebMD*. https://www.webmd.com/mental-health/news/20230811/suicides-us-reached-all-time-high-2022-cdc

54. Andrews, E. (2023, September 5). *8 reasons why Rome fell*. HISTORY. https://www.history.com/news/8-reasons-why-rome-fell

55. Shakil, I., & Scherer, S. (2023, April 19). Canadian federal workers strike over wages, work-from-home guarantees. *Reuters*. https://www.reuters.com/world/americas/some-155000-public-workers-canada-strike-over-pay-dispute-2023-04-19/

56. National Post Staff. (2023, September 11). Ironically, Canada ranked as the second best country in the world for quality of life. *Nationalpost*. https://nationalpost.com/news/canada-second-best-country-to-live-in

57. Government of Canada, Statistics Canada. (2023, June 19). *Canada's population reaches 40 million*. https://www.statcan.gc.ca/en/subjects-start/population_and_demography/40-million

58. Sachdeva, R. (2022, October 13). Affordability crisis: Why young Canadians are facing a "huge" wealth gap. *CTVNews*. https://www.ctvnews.ca/business/affordability-crisis-why-young-canadians-are-facing-a-huge-wealth-gap-1.6106343

59. Butler, C. (2023, March 15). Ontario's young adults are leaving the province in droves. The soaring cost of living is to blame. *CBC News*. https://www.cbc.ca/news/canada/london/ontario-alberta-move-migration-population-outflow-1.6778456#:~:text=Analysts%20blame%20the%20soaring%20cost%20of%201

iving%2C%20stagnant%20wages%20and,this%20large%20an%20exodus%20before.

60. Staff. (2023, October 27). *Food Banks Overwhelmed By Almost 2 Million Visits In One Month*. Kingsville Times. https://kingsvilletimes.ca/2023/10/food-banks-overwhelmed-by-almost-2-million-visits-in-one-month/#:~:text=Food%20Banks%20Overwhelmed%20By%20Almost%202%20Million%20Visits%20In%20One%20Month,-October%2027%2C%202023&text=Kirstin%20Beardsley%2C%20CEO%2C%20Food%20Banks,doors%20for%20the%20first%20time.

61. Pereira, A. P. B., Bloomberg News. (2022, August 29). Rents are so high in Toronto that students are living in homeless shelters. *Financialpost*. https://financialpost.com/real-estate/toronto-shelter-says-one-third-of-its-residents-are-students

62. Fifth Estate. (2022, October 11). Sold a Lie. *CBC*. https://www.cbc.ca/news/fifthestate/sold-a-lie-1.6612702

63. Hanrahan, L. (2022, June 2). Most Ontario renters choosing between food and paying rent: report. *STOREYS*. https://storeys.com/ontario-choose-paying-rent-food-report/

64. Marchesan, J. (2023, July 1). *Prime Minister Trudeau strikes optimistic tone in annual Canada Day message*. CityNews Toronto. https://toronto.citynews.ca/2023/07/01/justin-trudeau-canada-day-message/

65. *AutoTrader names Honda Civic best overall car in Canada*. (2021, November 16). Honda Canada Automobiles Newsroom. https://hondanews.ca/en-CA/hci-automobiles/releases/release-bc2bc74408027960dba69cafec1283d2-autotrader-names-honda-civic-best-overall-car-in-canada#:~:text=%E2%80%9CThere%20are%20many%20reasons%20why,Assistant%20Vice%20President%20Honda%20Canada.

66. *63% Of Canadians Have 'Given Up' On Buying Home*. (2022, April 30). Realty+, an Exchange4media Group Publication Is India's Leading Real Estate Monthly Magazine With Offices in Delhi, Mumbai and Bengaluru. https://www.rprealtyplus.com/amp/international/63-of-canadians-have-given-up-on-buying-home-105973.html

67. Klasing, A. (2016, June 7). Make it Safe. In *Human Rights Watch*. https://www.hrw.org/report/2016/06/07/make-it-safe/canadas-obligation-end-first-nations-water-crisis

68. Government of Canada, Department of Justice, Electronic Communications. (2023, January 20). *Missing and murdered Indigenous women and girls - JustFacts*. https://www.justice.gc.ca/eng/rp-pr/jr/jf-pf/2017/july04.html#:~:text=The%20rate%20of%20murdered%20Indigenous

%20women%20in%20Canada%20was%204.82%20per%20100%2C000.&text=The%20rate%20of%20murdered%20Indigenous%20women%20in%20Manitoba%20was%207.16,was%206.79%3B%20Saskatchewan%20was%206.01.&text=Footnote%207-,Due%20to%20the%20small%20numbers%2C%20comparing,should%20be%20done%20with%20caution.

69. *Jamaica | History, Population, Flag, Map, Capital, & Facts*. (2023, November 13). Encyclopedia Britannica. https://www.britannica.com/place/Jamaica/British-rule

70. Edun, A. M. (1947). INDIANS IN BRITISH GUIANA. *India Quarterly, 3(2), 170-173*. http://www.jstor.org/stable/45067444

71. Franklin, B. (1736). Definition of an ounce of prevention is worth a pound of cure. In Merriam-Webster Dictionary. https://www.merriam-webster.com/dictionary/an%20ounce%20of%20prevention%20is%20worth%20a%20pound%20of%20cure

72. Tabachnick, C. (2023, October 11). Hit in DNA database exonerates man 47 years after wrongful rape conviction. *CBS News*. https://www.cbsnews.com/news/leonard-mack-exonerated-47-years-after-wrongful-rape-conviction/

73. Damien Frost & Associates LLP, Professional Discipline and Health Insurance Lawyers. (2021, September 23). *Fraud over $5,000 - Toronto | Damien Frost & Associates LLP*. Professional Discipline and Health Insurance Lawyers. https://www.damienfrost.ca/fraud-over-5000-lawyer/#:~:text=Under%20the%20Criminal%20Code%20of,imprisonment%20up%20to%2014%20years.

74. Van Anders, S. M. (2012). Testosterone and sexual desire in healthy women and men. *Archives of Sexual Behavior, 41(6), 1471–1484*. https://doi.org/10.1007/s10508-012-9946-2

75. *House Prices Are Up: Should We Be Happy?* (2019, May 16). IMF. https://www.imf.org/en/Blogs/Articles/2019/05/16/blog-chart-of-the-week-house-prices-are-up-should-we-be-happy

76. Bremen, J. M. (2023, May 17). Why salary increases *Still* do not align with inflation. *Forbes*. https://www.forbes.com/sites/johnbremen/2023/05/17/why-salary-increases-still-do-not-align-with-inflation/?sh=272f4f5f5d0d

77. Radford, B. A. (2023, August 28). Jacksonville gunman who shot three dead left racist messages - police. *BBC News*. https://www.bbc.com/news/world-us-canada-66633186

78. Smith, S. D. (2021, November 12). *Volvo Says Manufacturing An Electric Car Generates 70 Percent More Emissions Than Its ICE Equivalent | Carscoops*. Carscoops. https://www.carscoops.com/2021/11/volvo-says-manufacturing-an-electric-car-generates-70-percent-more-emissions-than-its-petrol-equivalent/

79. Hayden, W. (2021, June 17). HISTORY: From horse to horsepower. *The News Herald*. https://www.thenewsherald.com/2011/01/05/history-from-horse-to-horsepower/

80. Energy, E. C. (2023, November 1). The shocking effect of electric car battery disposal on local and global public health. *Energy5*. https://energy5.com/the-shocking-effect-of-electric-car-battery-disposal-on-local-and-global-public-health#

81. Mambra, S. (2022, April 30). *Ocean pollution – 6 things that make it worse*. Marine Insight. https://www.marineinsight.com/environment/causes-and-effects-of-ocean-dumping/

82. Britannica, T. Editors of Encyclopaedia (2023, October 6). blood diamond. Encyclopedia Britannica. https://www.britannica.com/topic/blood-diamond

83. Cheema, S. (2021, July 8). Fish are getting high by eating human poop containing meth and it's not good. *Mashable SEA*. https://sea.mashable.com/science/16574/fish-are-getting-high-by-eating-human-poop-containing-meth-and-its-not-good

84. Gartner, K. (2016, October 13). *Consumerism, Mass Extinction and our Throw-Away Society | The Art Of*. https://www.theartof.com/articles/consumerism-mass-extinction-and-our-throw-away-society

85. Kramer, K. (2012). Sustainability, user experience, and design. In *Elsevier eBooks* (pp. 1–30). https://doi.org/10.1016/b978-0-12-387795-6.00001-9

86. MacMillan, A. (2023, August 21). 4 possible reasons why mental health is getting worse. *Health*. https://www.health.com/condition/depression/8-million-americans-psychological-distress#:~:text=Possible%20reasons%20why%20mental%20health%20is%20getting%20worse%20include%20factors,what%20you%20need%20to%20know.

87. *Vaccines save and extend lives - BIO*. (n.d.). BIO. https://archive.bio.org/articles/vaccines-save-and-extend-lives

88. Dinesh K. Singal, MD FACC FACP FSCAI. (n.d.). *What's behind the rise in heart attacks among young people?: Cardio Metabolic Institute: Multi-Specialty Group*. https://www.cminj.com/blog/whats-behind-the-rise-in-heart-attacks-among-young-people

89. Dr. Barton, S. (2022, June 16). *Is infertility on the rise?* CCRM Fertility. https://www.ccrmivf.com/blog/is-infertility-on-the-rise/#:~:text=Infertility%20rates%20are%20rising%2C%20according,according%20to%20the%20United%20Nations.

90. Walsh, B. (2013, October 21). *Why we don't care about saving our grandchildren from climate change | TIME.com*.

TIME.com. https://science.time.com/2013/10/21/why-we-dont-care-about-saving-our-grandchildren-from-climate-change/

91. Investigators, B. P. (2020, April 25). *The Thai girlfriend scam - Bangkok Investigators*. Bangkok Private Investigators. https://bangkokinvestigators.com/blog/the-thai-girlfriend-scam

92. Lauer, C. (2019, October 4). *Almost 1,700 priests and clergy accused of sex abuse are unsupervised*. NBC News. https://www.nbcnews.com/news/religion/nearly-1-700-priests-clergy-accused-sex-abuse-are-unsupervised-n1062396

93. Reynolds, E. (2015, May 20). Terrible news for short people. *News*. https://www.news.com.au/finance/work/careers/why-tall-people-earn-more-and-have-better-jobs/news-story/af0ac81f59ced89c2f5d9fb4b65a2c19

94. Obodovskiy, K. (2021, November 20). *The unique requirement of police forces around the world*. InTime. https://intime.com/industries/police/requirement-police-forces-around-world/

95. Bunn, C. (2022, March 4). *Report: Black people are still killed by police at a higher rate than other groups*. NBC News. https://www.nbcnews.com/news/nbcblk/report-black-people-are-still-killed-police-higher-rate-groups-rcna17169

96. Wilson, C., & Aguilar, B. (2020, June 22). Family identifies 62-year-old man killed in police-involved shooting in Malton. *CP24*. https://www.cp24.com/news/family-identifies-62-year-old-man-killed-in-police-involved-shooting-in-malton-1.4993356?cache=

97. Pazzanese, C., & Parsons, L. (2021, May 14). How unjust police killings damage the mental health of Black Americans. *Harvard Gazette*. https://news.harvard.edu/gazette/story/2021/05/how-unjust-police-killings-damage-the-mental-health-of-black-americans/

98. Dolittle, R. (2008, October 1). Ombudsman slams SIU bias. *Toronto Star*. https://www.thestar.com/news/ontario/ombudsman-slams-siu-bias/article_a74276d4-9333-56c1-8cb3-7571bf231778.html

99. *Changing Patterns of Divorce Sociology*. (n.d.). StudySmarter UK. https://www.studysmarter.co.uk/explanations/social-studies/families-and-households/changing-patterns-of-divorce-sociology/#:~:text=The%20three%20most%20important%20reasons,desertion%20are%20alternatives%20to%20divorce.

100. Dukakis, A. (2017, April 4). Child Marriage, Common In The Past, Persists Today. *Colorado Public Radio*. https://www.cpr.org/show-segment/child-marriage-common-in-the-past-persists-today/#:~:text=But%20it%20is%20also%20the,middle%20of%20the%20nineteenth%20century.

101. Riotta, C. (2016, February 5). *Where did the term "Ghosted" come from? Origin of the web's favorite term for abandonment.* Mic. https://www.mic.com/articles/134418/where-did-the-term-ghosted-come-from-origin-of-the-web-s-favorite-term-for-abandonment

102. Hughes, H. (2020, March 5). *We're Living Longer Than We Did 100 Years Ago, But Are We Actually Healthier? - Elizabeth Hughes M.D.* Elizabeth Hughes M.D. https://elizabethhughesmd.com/were-living-longer-are-we-actually-healthier/

103. Heaney, K. (2021, August 9). Why more people are having sex on the first Date - OkCupid Dating blog. *Medium.* https://theblog.okcupid.com/why-more-people-are-having-sex-on-the-first-date-7330ddbea30f

104. McCall, I. (2023, May 16). Why 80% of women only date 20% of men - Yard couch - medium. *Medium.* https://medium.com/yardcouch-com/new-study-shows-why-80-of-women-only-date-20-of-men-3f27432757ce

105. Desk, H. (2023, June 26). *(Video) Local Influencers Called Out For Faking Luxurious Lifestyle To Promote Business.* Hype MY. https://hype.my/2023/336371/video-local-influencers-called-out-for-faking-luxurious-lifestyle-to-promote-business/

106. Laskowski, N., & Tucci, L. (2023, November 13). *artificial intelligence (AI).* Enterprise AI. https://www.techtarget.com/searchenterpriseai/definition/AI-Artificial-Intelligence

107. Kahn, J. (2022, October 26). Inside 'Are We Dating the Same Guy,' the secret Facebook group where women review men they've dated. *Glamour.* https://www.glamour.com/story/are-we-dating-the-same-guy-facebook-group

108. Stodart, L., & Britt, T. (2023, November 4). *Best hookup apps and dating sites for casual sex: Updated for October 2023.* Mashable. https://mashable.com/roundup/best-hookup-apps

109. College of Family Physicians of Canada. (2018, March 1). *Are we losing the battle against sexually transmitted diseases in Canada?* PubMed Central (PMC). https://www.ncbi.nlm.nih.gov/pmc/articles/PMC5851395/

110. Pollok, S. (2023, June 28). What is a passport bro? The unconventional travel dating technique. *NZ Herald.* https://www.nzherald.co.nz/travel/what-is-a-passport-bro-the-unconventional-travel-dating-technique/DBAUXAJ6UNGZRFJTZ26HQ3O4AA/

111. Wrenn, D. H., Yi, J., & Zhang, B. (2019). House prices and marriage entry in China. *Regional Science and Urban Economics, 74,* 118–130. https://doi.org/10.1016/j.regsciurbeco.2018.12.001

112. Alvarez, P. (2022, July 14). *What does the global decline of the fertility rate look like?* World Economic

Forum. https://www.weforum.org/agenda/2022/06/global-decline-of-fertility-rates-visualised/

113. Supharta, K. (2023, October 6). *M'sian man has affair & impregnates married woman, court orders him to pay S$8,700 to husband.* Mothership.SG - News From Singapore, Asia and Around the World. https://mothership.sg/2023/10/man-cheating-pay-fine/

114. McManamon, P. (2022, October 10). *Financial help for single parents.* InCharge Debt Solutions. https://www.incharge.org/debt-relief/financial-help-single-moms-and-dads/

115. *How social media affects marriage & divorce - Stanley-Wallace Law.* (2018, August 16). Stanley-Wallace Law. https://stanley-wallacelaw.com/how-social-media-affects-divorce/#:~:text=Did%20you%20know%20that%20social,additional%20problems%20during%20a%20divorce.

116. Online, E. (2023, August 7). Costly vows, uncertain future: Study shows correlation between wedding spending and divorce rates. *The Economic Times.* https://economictimes.indiatimes.com/news/new-updates/costly-vows-uncertain-future-study-shows-correlation-between-wedding-spending-and-divorce-rates/articleshow/102490778.cms#

117. Hrustic, A. (2016, September 20). Why you make stupid decisions when you're horny. *Men's Health.* https://www.menshealth.com/sex-women/a19528870/stupid-decisions-when-horny/

118. DiNunno, G. (2010, February 19). Tiger Woods: "I felt I was entitled." *TVGuide.com.* https://www.tvguide.com/news/tiger-woods-felt-1015248/

119. Gupta, A. H., & Mazón, L. (2022, August 29). How love languages became a cultural phenomenon. *The New York Times.* https://www.nytimes.com/2022/08/27/well/family/love-languages-author.html#:~:text=Then%2C%20three%20decades%20ago%2C%20Gary,expressing%20and%20understanding%20love%2C%20Dr.

120. Hebert, R. (2022, February 17). *New York's Divorce Rate: Why Are So Many Couples Ending Their Marriages? - OnlineDivorceNY.com.* OnlineDivorceNY.com. https://onlinedivorceny.com/new-yorks-divorce-rate/

121. Correspondent, HT. (2009, May 26). Mother-in-law top reason for Malaysian Indian divorces: Study. *Hindustan Times.* https://www.hindustantimes.com/india/mother-in-law-top-reason-for-malaysian-indian-divorces-study/story-aobSwXjZSrLod0LHGFOsFM.html

122. Milden, D., Hall, L., & Davis, L. M. (2023, September 13). Inflation keeps on trucking, thanks to high gas prices. *CNET.* https://www.cnet.com/personal-finance/banking/inflation-keeps-on-trucking-thanks-to-high-gas-prices/

123. Sullivan, M. (2018, May 23). Divorce Is Prohibited In The Philippines, But Moves Are Underway To Legalize
It. *NPR*. https://www.npr.org/sections/parallels/2018/05/23/613335232/divorce-is-prohibited-in-the-philippines-but-moves-are-underway-to-legalize-it

124. Siva, S. (2022, September 26). Yes, I got divorced. No, do not call me a divorcee. *Vogue India*. https://www.vogue.in/culture-and-living/content/yes-i-got-divorced-no-do-not-call-me-a-divorcee-indian-marriages

125. Admin, M. (2022, December 3). *Divorce in Islam - Al Rashid Mosque*. https://alrashidmosque.ca/divorce/

126. Bishop, K. (2022, July 26). Why women file for divorce more than men. *BBC Worklife*. https://www.bbc.com/worklife/article/20220511-why-women-file-for-divorce-more-than-men

127. *Sharing principle | Practical Law*. (n.d.). Practical Law. Thomas Reuters. https://uk.practicallaw.thomsonreuters.com/2-538-0225?transitionType=Default&contextData=(sc.Default)&firstPage=true

128. Government of Canada, Department of Justice, Electronic Communications. (2022, March 7). *Department of Justice - About spousal support*. https://www.justice.gc.ca/eng/fl-df/spousal-epoux/ss-pae.html

129. Novack, J. (2015, January 30). Getting married? Got assets? Read this first. *Forbes*. https://www.forbes.com/sites/janetnovack/2015/01/30/getting-married-got-assets-read-this-first/?sh=4ac248374053

130. Thompson, S. (2023, April 17). Wife of Moroccan soccer star loses divorce settlement as fortune is in his mother's name. *Fox News*. https://www.foxnews.com/sports/wife-moroccan-soccer-star-loses-divorce-settlement-fortune-mothers-name

131. Boland, J. (2015, August 20). National Post View: Throwing cheaters under the bus. *Nationalpost*. https://nationalpost.com/opinion/national-post-view-throwing-cheaters-under-the-bus

132. Wikipedia contributors. (2023, November 20). *List of Generation Z slang*. Wikipedia. https://en.wikipedia.org/wiki/List_of_Generation_Z_slang#Body_count

133. *Over half of U.S. teens have had sexual intercourse by age 18, new report shows*. (2018, June 22). Centers for Disease Control and Prevention. https://www.cdc.gov/nchs/pressroom/nchs_press_releases/2017/201706_NSFG.htm

134. Green Hill. (2021, September 17). *Understanding Trauma and Addiction - Green Hill Recovery*. Green Hill Recovery. https://greenhillrecovery.com/understanding-trauma-and-addiction/#:~:text=Emotional%20Trauma%20and%20Addiction&text=Things%20such%20as%20bullying%20or,deal%20with%20PTSD%2C%20or%20escape.

135. American Lung Association. (n.d.). *10 of the Worst Diseases Smoking Causes | State of Tobacco Control.* https://www.lung.org/research/sotc/by-the-numbers/10-worst-diseases-smoking-causes

136. Rojas, C. R. (2021, July 8). How stress increases dementia risk. *Orlando Health.* https://www.orlandohealth.com/content-hub/how-stress-increases-dementia-risk

137. *To What Extent Does Childhood Trauma Influence One To Become A Serial Killer? - Edubirdie.* (2023, August 7). Edubirdie. https://edubirdie.com/examples/to-what-extent-does-childhood-trauma-influence-one-to-become-a-serial-killer/#:~:text=Serial%20Killers%20Who%20Had%20Childhood%20Trauma,-A%20traumatic%20childhood&text=This%20is%20especially%20true%20for,(Fiona%20Guy%2C%202020).

138. *The Mental health Impact of Child Abuse | McLean Hospital.* (2023, August 18). https://www.mcleanhospital.org/essential/effects-child-abuse#:~:text=Childhood%20abuse%20has%20mental%20and,of%20life%20beyond%20the%20abuse.

139. JRailPass. (2021, June 4). *Japan train etiquette: Tips for understanding Japanese manners.* Japan Rail Pass Travel Blog | JRailPass. https://www.jrailpass.com/blog/japan-train-etiquette#:~:text=Many%20people%20use%20their%20mobile,cannot%20be%20heard%20by%20others.

140. *Foster care - Child Welfare Information Gateway.* (n.d.). https://www.childwelfare.gov/topics/outofhome/foster-care/#:~:text=Foster%20care%20(also%20known%20as,or%20with%20unrelated%20foster%20parents.

141. Grey, S., & Peleschuk, D. (2023, September 19). Corruption accusations continue to plague top Zelenskiy aides. *Reuters.* https://www.reuters.com/world/europe/graft-accusations-dog-top-zelenskiy-aides-2023-09-19/

142. Source, C. U. (2022, April 9). Thinking about buying a car? Here's what auto experts say you need to know. *CNBC.* https://www.cnbc.com/2022/04/09/thinking-about-buying-a-car-heres-what-experts-say-you-need-to-know.html#:~:text=That%20makes%20it%20the%20second,credit%20histories%20and%20lower%20savings.

143. Howard, D. C. (2010, February 22). Planned obsolescence: 8 products designed to fail. *Popular Mechanics.* https://www.popularmechanics.com/technology/g202/planned-obsolescence-460210/

144. McLeod, D. (2023, October 30). *What is a white Lie? – Definition, origin and examples*. GRAMMARIST. https://grammarist.com/usage/white-lie/

145. Buncombe, A. (2017, January 10). Thousands call for release of man who shot dead his daughter's rapist | The Independent. *The Independent*. https://www.independent.co.uk/news/world/americas/father-pardon-jay-manor-shot-dead-daughter-sex-attacker-raymond-earl-brooks-release-alabama-jailed-40-years-prison-sentence-a7517576.html

146. Brumer-Smith, L. (2023, August 8). *My Contractor Stole My Money and Ran—Here's What I Learned, So You Don't Make the Same Mistakes*. Real Estate News & Insights | realtor.com®. https://www.realtor.com/advice/home-improvement/my-contractor-stole-my-money-and-ran-heres-what-i-learned-so-you-dont-make-the-same-mistakes/

147. Ohrnberger, J., Fichera, E., & Sutton, M. (2017). The relationship between physical and mental health: A mediation analysis. *Social Science & Medicine, 195*, 42–49. https://doi.org/10.1016/j.socscimed.2017.11.008

148. Park, A. (2017, August 7). Why Sunlight Is So Good For You. *Time*. https://time.com/4888327/why-sunlight-is-so-good-for-you/

149. *Life expectancy by country and in the world (2023) - Worldometer*. https://www.worldometers.info/demographics/life-expectancy/

150. Pettit, H. (2018, September 17). Robots and artificial intelligence will take over HALF of all tasks in the workplace by 2025. *Mail Online*. https://www.dailymail.co.uk/sciencetech/article-6175599/Machines-handle-half-workplace-tasks-2025.html

151. Nunez, K., & Lamoreux, K. (2023, June 20). *What is the purpose of sleep?* Healthline. https://www.healthline.com/health/why-do-we-sleep#why-do-we-sleep

152. TIMESOFINDIA.COM. (2022, September 7). 7 most harmful chemicals added to common foods. *The Times of India*. https://timesofindia.indiatimes.com/life-style/food-news/7-most-harmful-chemicals-added-to-common-foods/photostory/94048229.cms

153. Body Details. (2021, September 22). *Exercises to flush out toxins & cleanse your body*. https://www.bodydetails.com/blog/exercise-flush-toxins/#:~:text=Exercising%20quickens%20breathing%2C%20promotes%20blood,nodes%20to%20do%20their%20job.

154. *Exercise and stress: Get moving to manage stress*. (2022, August 3). Mayo Clinic. https://www.mayoclinic.org/healthy-lifestyle/stress-management/in-depth/exercise-and-stress/art-20044469#

155. Research, C. F. D. E. A. (2022, August 8). *Finding and Learning about Side Effects (adverse reactions)*. U.S. Food And Drug Administration. https://www.fda.gov/drugs/information-consumers-and-patients-drugs/finding-and-learning-about-side-effects-adverse-

reactions#:~:text=However%2C%20both%20prescription%20and%20over,possibly%20related%20to%20a%20drug.

156. Desk, L. (2023, February 16). Cuddling not only feels good, it also has oodles of health benefits. *The Indian Express*. https://indianexpress.com/article/lifestyle/health/cuddling-health-benefits-better-immune-system-bond-improve-partner-science-8447076/

157. Government of Canada, Department of Justice, Electronic Communications. (2021, July 7). *Cannabis Legalization and regulation*. https://www.justice.gc.ca/eng/cj-jp/cannabis/

158. Reporter, G. S. (2017, December 19). Australian man in Bali charged with drug offences that can carry death penalty. *The Guardian*. https://www.theguardian.com/world/2017/dec/19/australian-man-in-bali-charged-with-drug-offences-that-can-carry-death-penalty

159. *Consumer Medicine Information - Prozac*. (2023, September). Medsinfo.com.au. https://medsinfo.com.au/consumer-information/document/Prozac_CMI

160. Do American parents raise the world's most spoiled kids? (2012, July 5*). CBS News*. https://www.cbsnews.com/newyork/news/does-america-raise-the-worlds-most-spoiled-kids/

161. Graham, J., Meindl, P., Beall, E., Johnson, K., & Zhang, L. (2016). Cultural differences in moral judgment and behavior, across and within societies. *Current Opinion in Psychology, 8*, 125-130. https://doi.org/10.1016/j.copsyc.2015.09.007

162. Pedersen, T. (2022, July 14). *What do therapists have to report?* Psych Central. https://psychcentral.com/health/what-do-therapists-have-to-report

163. Stewart, B. (2015, May 6). 22 Brutal crash tests that changed the way cars are built. *Popular Mechanics*. https://www.popularmechanics.com/cars/g2005/22-brutal-crash-tests-video/

164. *L.A. man wrongly imprisoned for decades is declared innocent after DNA evidence points to a different suspect*. (2023, March 2). NBC News. https://www.nbcnews.com/news/us-news/l-man-wrongly-imprisoned-decades-declared-innocent-dna-evidence-points-rcna72843

165. Jardina, A., & Piston, S. (2023). Trickle-Down racism: Trump's effect on whites' racist dehumanizing attitudes. *Current Research in Ecological and Social Psychology, 5*, 100158. https://doi.org/10.1016/j.cresp.2023.100158

166. *Child marriage: a violation of child rights*. (n.d.). Save the Children. https://www.savethechildren.org/us/charity-stories/child-marriage-a-violation of child-rights

167. Professional, C. C. M. (2023, September 18). *Dissociative amnesia*. Cleveland Clinic. https://my.clevelandclinic.org/health/diseases/9789-dissociative-amnesia

168. Sissons, B. (2023, August 22). *What is the link between trauma and schizophrenia?* Medical News Today. https://www.medicalnewstoday.com/articles/trauma-and-schizophrenia

169. Understanding Voices. (2020, November 25). *Voices and trauma - Understanding Voices.* Understanding Voices - Information for People Who Hear Voices and Those Who Support Them. https://understandingvoices.com/exploring-voices/why-do-people-hear-voices/voices-and-trauma/#:~:text=Some%20kinds%20of%20trauma%20have,can%20be%20related%20to%20trauma.

170. Alyssa. (2020, July 29). *The Effects of Trauma on the Brain | Mental Health blog.* Mental Health Program at Banyan Treatment Centers. https://www.banyanmentalhealth.com/2020/05/12/effects-of-trauma-on-the-brain/

171. Barrell, A. (2023, September 25). *Why are my hands shaking? Causes, is it normal, and remedies.* Medical News Today. https://www.medicalnewstoday.com/articles/322195

172. Abraham, M. (2020, October 10). *Slurred speech from Anxiety: Causes and treatments.* Calm Clinic. https://www.calmclinic.com/anxiety/symptoms/slurred-speech

173. Scott, E., PhD. (2021, October 7). *How stress works with and against your memory.* Verywell Mind. https://www.verywellmind.com/stress-and-your-memory-4158323#:~:text=Stress%20can%20affect%20the%20type,we%20perceived%20at%20the%20time.

174. *Where did dinosaurs live? | U.S. Geological Survey.* (2020, March 27). https://www.usgs.gov/faqs/where-did-dinosaurs-live#:~:text=Dinosaurs%20lived%20on%20all%20of,this%20supercontinent%20slowly%20broke%20apart.

175. *Hypothetical Planet X - NASA Science.* (n.d.). https://science.nasa.gov/solar-system/planet-x/

176. Chandler, N. (2023, October 20). *10 Scientific Questions We Can't Answer Yet.* HowStuffWorks. https://science.howstuffworks.com/innovation/scientific-experiments/10-questions-science-cant-answer-yet.htm

177. G-Innovative. (2022, March 22). *What is Carbon Fiber? | Innovative Composite Engineering.* Innovative Composite Engineering. https://www.innovativecomposite.com/what-is-carbon-fiber/

178. Challenger, C. (2023, January 24). 10 Mental Health Benefits of Owning a Cat - MEOW Foundation. *MEOW Foundation - Calgary Cat Rescue - Cat and Kitten Adoption.* https://meowfoundation.com/10-mental-health-benefits-of-owning-a-cat-how-our-feline-friends-make-our-lives-happier-

healthier/#:~:text=Studies%20have%20shown%20that%20cats%20have%20a%20calming%2C%20stress%2Dreducing,can%20significantly%20elevate%20our%20mood.

179. Bence, S. (2023, June 14). *All about grounding: techniques to connect to nature.* Verywell Health. https://www.verywellhealth.com/grounding-7494652

180. Syed. (2023, February 1). *Emotional stress and heart Attack | London Heart Clinic.* London Heart Clinic. https://theheartclinic.london/blog/emotional-stress-and-heart-attack-awareness-and-prevention/#:~:text=Can%20emotional%20stress%20cause%20a,can%20be%20just%20as%20deadly.

181. Yeebo, Y. (2011, June 26). Soaring costs force some renters to choose between shelter and food. *HuffPost.* https://www.huffpost.com/entry/rent-vs-buy_n_852779

182. *Rose Island - The story of a micronation.* (n.d.). https://www.rose-island.co/

183. Seabury, C. (2023, May 25). *How interest rates affect the U.S. markets.* Investopedia. https://www.investopedia.com/articles/stocks/09/how-interest-rates-affect-markets.asp#:~:text=However%2C%20when%20rates%20are%20too,sustainability%20of%20the%20economic%20expansion.

184. Kenton, W. (2022, January 12). *Wage Push Inflation: Definition, Causes, and Examples.* Investopedia. https://www.investopedia.com/terms/w/wage-push-inflation.asp

<u>Notes</u>